SPIES IN BRITISH CONTROLLED SINGAPORE

Dr Edward J. Drea

SPIES IN BRITISH CONTROLLED SINGAPORE

Policing the Japanese, 1921–1941

The Asian Studies Collection

Collection Editor
Dr Dong Wang

LPP

For Rika

First published in 2023 by Lived Places Publishing.

British Library Cataloguing in Publication Data
A CIP record for this book is available from the British Library

ISBN: 9781915271723 (pbk)
ISBN: 9781915271747 (ePDF)
ISBN: 9781915271730 (ePUB)

The rights of Edward J. Drea to be identified as the Author of this work have been asserted by him in accordance with the Copyright, Design and Patents Act 1988.

Cover design by Fiachra McCarthy
Book design by Rachel Trolove of Twin Trail Design
Typeset by Newgen Publishing UK

Lived Places Publishing
Long Island
New York 11789
www.livedplacespublishing.com

Abstract

Before December 1941, Singapore was the site of a major naval base for the occupying British. As tensions increased between the imperial powers of Japan and Britain, Japanese expatriates living in Singapore became the focus of both the British and Japanese governments in the struggle for control and power, resulting in further marginalization and suspicion of resident Japanese by the Singapore authorities who othered the communities in which they lived.

Based on British police records and Japanese military records of the time, this book explores how people were used—sometimes without their knowledge and consent—as spies and intelligence agents.

Keywords

Military history; war; espionage; colonialism; empire; migration; expatriate; Malaya; East Asia; Southeast Asia

Contents

Preface

This book originated in my curiosity about the Japanese whom the colonial security police identified as spies. Were the Japanese residents of Singapore enemy agents and, if so, what did they accomplish? From a different perspective, how effective were the colonial police in controlling espionage? Answering these questions meant addressing the combination of interaction between races and cultures in a colonial setting during a period of growing international tensions that influenced Singapore's domestic policy. British colonial authorities viewed all Japanese with suspicion, but most Japanese residents, while sympathetic to Tokyo, were not involved in espionage or subversion. However, though British concerns may have been exaggerated, Japanese spies did operate within the expatriate community, organized around Singapore's Japanese consulate that engaged in espionage and subversion. Providing both sides of the story may remove some of the many myths about Singapore's spies.

My thanks to the following scholars for reading earlier drafts of this manuscript: Raymond Callahan, John Carland, Brian Farrell, Roger Jeans, Gerhard Krebs, and Steve Rabson. I am indebted to Professor Dong Wang for her guidance.

Learning objectives

- Understand the different roles of Japanese civilian residents and Japanese military officers and diplomatic officials in Singapore.
- Understand the relationship between the colonial police in Singapore and the Colonial Office.
- Understand how the Japanese government manipulated Japanese residents of Singapore.
- Be aware of the evolving British attitude toward suspected espionage during the 1920s and 1930s.

Introduction

What role, if any, the Japanese expatriate community played in the collapse of British Malay states has provoked controversy since 1942. Early postwar versions insisted that clandestine Japanese spies posing as businessmen, correspondents, fishermen, photographers, and visitors from Japan were in large measure responsible for Britain's disastrous Malayan campaign, which culminated in the loss of Fortress Singapore in early 1942. Later accounts dismissed notions of a treacherous Japanese fifth column and attributed British defeat to combinations of ineptitude, unpreparedness, and racism. These later accounts were the source of ridicule of British authorities for attributing nefarious aims to the innocuous daily activities of Japanese residents of Malaya in order to conjure up visions of a colony-wide spy ring.

Put differently, British colonial authorities viewed all Japanese nationals with suspicion. The Singapore colonial police and British military representatives repeatedly sought broader powers of arrest and proposed mass internment of Japanese residents of the colony. Just as consistently, London rejected such extreme recommendations, citing precedents of imperial governance rooted in the rule of law. Colonial administrators' near-obsessive mistrust of the resident Japanese blinded them to the rising nationalism among indigenous Malays, whom many British colonists believed were favorably disposed to their "colonial masters."

The evidence shows that most Japanese residents, while sympathetic to Tokyo, were not directly involved in espionage or subversion. However, although British concerns were overwrought, Japanese spies did live and work within the expatriate community; they included respected senior bureaucrats and successful businessmen, rugged fishermen and small shopkeepers, male and female service workers, newspaper reporters, and so forth, and were loosely coordinated by Japan's Singapore consulate. For their part, Singapore's Japanese expatriates enjoyed Tokyo's strong support and Japan's Foreign Ministry was quick to complain about British treatment of its residents, lodging diplomatic protests or veiled threats of retaliation for perceived injustices. Simultaneously, the Japanese consulate in Singapore was exploiting the Japanese community by using many residents as unwitting or informal accomplices to its ongoing subversion campaign.

Japan's Singapore consulate was the hub of Japanese intelligence gathering in Southeast Asia. At first it relied on open-sources—newspapers, official publications and announcements, and firsthand observation—to provide intelligence to Tokyo. During the 1920s, the Japanese consulate worked with its naval attachés to gather mainly open-source intelligence about the emerging Singapore naval base. Such activity was a recognized, and grudgingly accepted, practice of all nations' diplomatic and consular posts, so long as it did not stray into illegal activity such as espionage or subversion. By the mid-1930s, however, certain Japanese residents of Singapore were actively engaged in clandestine espionage: the illicit acquisition of secret information. The shift caught the British unprepared, and a combination of law (all Singapore residents received equal protections) and London's own secret services (who determined that the benefits of releasing damning evidence of Japanese espionage operations did not outweigh the risks of compromising their sources) hampered a comprehensive response. These factors also governed British reactions to what might be termed Japan's espionage surge during 1940 and 1941.

Spying, by nature, is secret. Interpretations or opinions about clandestine influences on overall national success or failure are usually conditioned by external factors and extrapolated from results because so few know the hidden inside story. One likely reason the extent of Japanese espionage in Singapore prior to 1942 remains a contented topic is that the British and Japanese got rid of much of their official documentation. With the Japanese at Singapore's gates in February 1942, British police destroyed most of their own classified files rather than allow them to fall into enemy hands. Similarly, following Japan's surrender in the late summer of 1945, rumor spread that the victorious Allies intended to execute any Japanese who had engaged in spying or intelligence work, leading Japanese soldiers or petty officials to burn thousands of official military or diplomatic documents to eliminate evidence of incriminating conduct. The historical record on both sides is consequently incomplete and important gaps still remain.

Insofar as is possible, I have relied on contemporary records, both British and Japanese, to offer an accurate, if necessarily incomplete, account of what happened at a specific time and place. Because all the British documents cited are available at The National Archives, Kew repository, I cite these in the narrative in the pattern TNA, file number, digital frame number. Thus, TNA, KV3/426, 9 refers to the ninth digitized frame (not page) of file 426 from The National Archives. As for Japanese language documentation, the Japan Center for Asian Records (JCAR) reference number will guide a reader to the document or the file holding the document. I offer detailed titles of these documents in my "Notes" chapter because the information from those primary sources enables us to better appreciate contemporary British and Japanese thinking and acting during that unsettled era.

Singapore: The imperial city

Pre-Second World War British Malaya consisted of the British governed Straits Settlements—Singapore, Malacca, and Penang—as a Crown Colony, administered by a governor who answered to the Colonial Office. The British also indirectly administered the Federated and Unfederated Malay states. Singapore was a polyglot pastiche of Malay, Chinese, Indian, and Western European culture. Socially, it was bifurcated along racial lines between the Westerners and the others. The gleaming white buildings, well-tended city center, and plentiful green open spaces were typical of a Western colonial city. The privileged Europeans lived along Orchard Road in well-tended homes that were maintained by servants, and frequented the city's better shops, clubs, games, and garden parties. The others lived in intentionally segregated sectors: the Chinese to the city center's west and south, Malays and Arabs to its north, and Indians to its east.

Singapore was a bustling trading and commercial port whose busy harbor and waterfront exemplified its prominence as the hub of maritime trade in Southeast Asia. Ships brought cargoes, people, and capital. Commerce and trade thrived. Business was booming for contractors, planters, and retailers. Singapore's cinemas and dance cabarets were packed nightly as "The Bright Young Things ... were having the time of their lives"[1] (TNA, KV3/426, 65). Life was good, social status mattered more than unpleasant international realities, and most British residents convinced themselves "that nothing on earth could ever disturb the peace in the vast British Empire" (Frei, 2004, pp. 23–24).

To ensure tranquility amidst diversity, British civil authorities had organized the Criminal Investigation Division (CID) within the Straits Settlement Police in 1915 to keep track of subversive Indian nationalists. CID's name changed during the 1920s to Special Branch and its internal security mission was extended to the suppression of communist subversion, mainly within the rapidly growing Chinese community. Beginning in the mid-1930s, Singapore's resident Japanese population attracted greater Special Branch police attention.

By the late 1930s, perhaps 6,000 Japanese people resided in British Malaya, about half of whom resided in Singapore. Their numbers were infinitesimal compared to the colony's 5.5 million people, a figure that included the 750,000 living in Singapore, almost all of whom were Chinese, Indian, or Malay. But to the 18,000 mainly British Europeans who ran and ruled the colony, the Japanese population appeared threateningly large, especially because the Japanese residents clustered in distinct and close-knit communities whose very insularity magnified their presence to outsiders[2] (McCormick, 2006; Tsu, n.d.; Wigmore, 1957, p. 64n6).

In fact, Malaya's tiny Japanese population was on the decline; in the 1920s because of the post-war economic depression and in the 1930s because British regulations on the Japanese-dominated fishing industry coupled with previous restrictions on rubber production and foreign ownership of land forced many Japanese businesses to close and workers to leave. By 1939, the Japanese owned just eight plantations (down from 23 in 1921), which employed 112 Japanese workers (down from 521). Japanese businessmen still operated tin and iron mines and several Japanese-owned rubber plantations held out in northwestern Malaya and Jahore. Japanese trading companies had established themselves in Singapore and the two larger cities Georgetown and Kuala Lumpur on the Malaya peninsula. Smaller Japanese communities were scattered across Malaya, working as shopkeepers, barbers, clerks, photographers, innkeepers, salesmen, and so forth (Shimazu, 1993, pp. 63–87; Allen, 1991, p. 113; Bridges, 1986, p. 23; Everest-Phillips, 2007, pp. 243–244).

Most of Singapore's Japanese—fishermen, shopkeepers, entertainers, laborers, office employees, merchants, housewives, and children—crowded together in a trapezoid shaped area that encompassed a six-by-two block neighborhood north of the Singapore River, squeezed close to the southern edge of the Arab-Malay sector and on the wrong side of the social tracks. The posh city center government and office buildings nearby, with manicured gardens and wide boulevards, contrasted with Central Avenue (*Chūō dōri* to Japanese residents), which was bordered on both sides by a hodgepodge of Japanese-owned hotels and ryokans, restaurants and bars, markets and emporiums, and specialty shops and department stores. Closer to the waterfront and just off *Chūō dōri* was the Japanese-operated red-light district, crammed into the packed residential lanes. Wealthier Japanese businessmen, professionals, and diplomats lived in better neighborhoods like nearby Oxley Rise but retained close ties with the larger Japanese community.

Race, culture, and language added to the mutual misapprehension between the British and the Japanese that had been conjuring up British suspicions of a "Yellow Peril" since the late 19th century. Japan's initial commercial expansion into the region had fueled anxieties that the newcomers were the vanguard of a future invasion. The Japanese indeed welcomed business from everyone, and offered unfailingly polite service, but rarely socialized with outsiders once the workday ended. Their apartness compounded this mistrust. By the early 1930s, British intelligence lamented that "All Japanese, male or female, kept very much to themselves; they speak a language which hardly anyone in the Peninsula knows even a little of... It is therefore extremely difficult to find any chink in the armour of reserve and exclusiveness which they wear" (Lam, 2012).

Conventional Western stereotypes depicted Japanese as sneaky, untrustworthy, and disloyal, making them a menace to the colony sentiments. This was encapsulated in an April 1941 military report that concluded "espionage will continue so long as the Japanese, who are all born spies, are in the country"[3] (TNA, KV3/426, 117). Such were the commonplace perceptions wherever Japanese people migrated: Australia, Canada, the Netherlands East Indies, and the United States (Best, 2002, pp. 15–17, 47). Even as the Japanese population in Singapore declined, their presence became ever more sinister to the British because of Singapore's newfound strategic prominence and Japan's military expansion.

The British cabinet's decision to cut military expenditures, made in order to reduce the nation's massive First World War-incurred debt, unintentionally expanded Singapore's strategic role during the interwar era. In August 1919, cabinet members adopted the ten-year rule for defense spending, assuming that because no major war would occur for the next ten years and determining their budgets accordingly[4] (TNA, CAB 23/15/31). New naval shipbuilding had come to an end, but Britain still had worldwide commitments that required fleets in both hemispheres. Then-ally Japan had filled in for the British navy in Asian waters during the First World War. However, post-war rivalry between Japan and the United States forced Great Britain to choose between allies, and by the summer of 1921 London accepted that the Anglo-Japanese alliance, admittedly of declining importance for both nations during the previous decade, could not be renewed.

Japan's post-war intervention in Siberia, oversight of mandated islands in the western Pacific, aggressive commercial penetration of traditional British and American markets in Asia, and ambitious naval building program heightened London's concerns about Tokyo's ambitions. The cabinet approved the Admiralty's recommendation to expand the small existing naval base in Singapore in mid-June 1921, just a few weeks before accepting Washington's invitation to participate in a forthcoming American-sponsored conference on naval limitations (Callahan, 1974, pp. 73–77).

The Washington Naval Conference (November 12, 1921–February 6, 1922) is predominantly remembered for the major participants' agreement to reduce capital ships on a pro-rata basis, but attendees also approved a non-fortification clause that restricted the Pacific naval powers—Great Britain, Japan, and the United States—from building or improving fortifications or naval bases on any of their island possessions except for Singapore, Hawaii, and Japan's home islands. A major Japanese objective was to prevent the United States from strengthening Guam and the Philippines, thereby eliminating their use as advance bases for the U.S. Navy (Evans & Peattie, 1997, p. 197; Yamamoto, 2016, pp. 54–55).

The agreed-upon reductions on top of the ten-year rule further complicated British security commitments to protect Australia and New Zealand. The Admiralty lacked sufficient warships to maintain even a peacetime fleet in East Asian waters. Without a fleet in East Asia, in the event of a crisis London would have to dispatch a fleet from European waters, making the development of a major naval base at Singapore essential to supporting and sustaining maritime operations. This strategy, encapsulated in the slogan "Main Fleet to Singapore," was a cost-effective though strategically flawed solution because no one could explain what would happen in the case that Britain was simultaneously involved in a European crisis. When questions later arose about the strategy, naval authorities disregarded concerns of simultaneous crises or simply left questions of Singapore's role if a main fleet was unavailable unanswered (Callahan, 1974, pp. 77–78; Farrell, 2015, pp. 34–40).

Britain and Japan did not turn into overnight enemies following the official termination of the Anglo-Japanese alliance in 1923. Throughout the mid-1920s, the British saw no immediate Japanese threat to Singapore from the sea and believed a ground attack from the Malaya peninsula impossible because the monsoon season made amphibious landings on the east coast unrealistic while jungle and swamp rendered overland movement by large ground forces unthinkable (Yamamoto, 2016, p. 207). The Imperial Japanese Army, focused on an emerging Soviet Union, shared the British view that the peninsula's topography, limited road and rail networks, and equatorial climate rendered an overland attack on Singapore unimaginable. Japan's revised 1923 imperial defense policy made no mention of Britain as a hypothetical opponent. Consequently, the Japanese military staffs prepared no contingency plans for an Anglo-Japanese conflict, though Japanese naval intelligence did take a professional interest in the expanding naval base, and the British suspected that Japanese fishing boats, crewed by Japanese naval officers, were collecting intelligence around Singapore's sea approaches. Singapore Island, however, offered precious little in the way of military significance during most of the 1920s, except for the sight of large work gangs employing thousands of unskilled, low-waged Indian and Malayan laborers fitfully clearing the land for the new base and building rudimentary structures (History, 2014; Liew, 2006, p. 418).

Preliminary work to expand the Singapore naval base began in January 1924 with land clearance, but the following month, the newly elected Labour government suspended all work on the project. With the return to power of the Conservatives, that

November work began again from scratch, but converting the jungled swampland into a stable base bedeviled the engineering effort, and site preparation continued for almost five years. By March 1929, the preparatory work was finally complete and a floating dock, manufactured in Britain and towed to Singapore, was in place. Contracts were let for future work, notably the graving dock to be completed within seven years. That June, the ruling Labour Party again slowed base development. A compromise between Labour and the Conservatives the following year enabled construction on the graving dock to proceed, but postponed all other projects such as airbases, docks, and defensive works for five years (DesRoisers, 1966, Ch VI; Farrell, 2015, pp. 32–34).

The Japanese embassy in London provided the Foreign Ministry in Tokyo with the publicly available 1930 House of Commons interpellations regarding the Singapore project[5] (JCAR Ref. No. C05021115700). The Singapore consulate likewise forwarded local press reports the following April when notifying Tokyo that construction had ceased on the Changi defensive works that guarded the entrance of the eastern Johore channel[6] (JCAR Ref. No. C05021557000). The Foreign Ministry routinely forwarded such reports to the vice-minister of the navy. The diplomats' reliance on open sources suggests that little Japanese espionage activity was underway, at least in Singapore.

The writing on the wall for the British Chiefs of Staff appeared during Japan's military intervention in Shanghai, Republic of China, in early 1932. Tokyo's brazen assault on the commercial center of Western interests in China compelled the Chiefs to admit that Britain could not militarily resist Japanese aggression in East Asia[7] (TNA, CAB 24/229 & CAB 23/70/19). That summer, the British War Office ordered immediate planning to strengthen Singapore's coastal defenses, with actual work starting not later than the end of 1934. As fortress construction became more technically sophisticated, British authorities brought in higher-skilled workers from India (the belief was that Malays were incompetent and that the Indian workers were more highly skilled) on a more permanent basis to maintain the emerging infrastructure (Liew, 2006, p. 418). Coastal batteries were operational by August 1934, reinforced by the transfer of a heavy artillery battery and anti-aircraft weapons from India (Maurice-Jones, 2012, pp. 210–211). The British made an official announcement of the transfers in November, which the Japanese consul in Singapore duly forwarded to Tokyo[8] (JCAR Ref. No. C05023479600). As Anglo-Japanese relations worsened during the early 1930s and base construction accelerated, the naval facilities and air bases materializing on Singapore Island attracted Japanese diplomats and retired naval officers, who launched the first proven Japanese espionage operation in Malaya. This amateurish spy ring relied upon untrained Japanese resident "secret agents" who, whatever else they were—business executives, drunks, doctors, sex workers, and so on—were not trained spies. The result was a hair-brained conspiracy concocted by resident Japanese in Singapore to get their hands on the naval base's secrets.

1
The first spy scandal

In early March 1934, a naval officer from a visiting Japanese squadron gave an inflammatory anti-British speech at Singapore's Malay Club. Japanese resident Kokubo Hiromichi enthusiastically translated the remarks into Malay for the audience. His fervor brought him the renewed attention of Special Branch detectives, who were already questioning Kokubo's repeated attempts to contact visiting Japanese officials. The Special Branch now placed him under police surveillance[9] (TNA, KV3/415, 48, 89, 96).

Kokubo had arrived in Singapore in January 1917 where he worked briefly as a salesclerk. For several years he knocked about Malaya, working as a clerk before returning to Singapore in 1920 where he eventually opened a small metal engraving shop just off *Chūō dōri*. He was married with four children[10] (TNA, KV3/416, 56). Various police reports described him as a "low class Japanese" of "poor repute," not very bright, and a "drunken boaster not even trusted by his own side"[11] (TNA, KV3/415, 87). Kokubo flaunted his contempt by distributing anti-British propaganda, mixing with petty criminals and grifters who offered to sell him information of military importance, and trawling Royal Air Force (RAF) base employees and servicemen for intelligence[12] (TNA, KV3/415, 96). Heavy drinking, wild exaggerations, and wishful fantasies combined with gullibility made him an easy mark for Special Branch. A few months later a shady police informer designated "M.6," a Sumatran political refugee of dubious reliability, approached Kokubo through one of his shop's employees. The two hit it off. Kokubo thought he had found a kindred anti-British spirit, and "M.6" believed that Kokubo had the "big money" that he constantly bragged about. Based on "M-6's" accounts, Special Branch detectives began intercepting Kokubo's mail.

In early August, Kokubo introduced "M.6" to Ohki Shoji, a newspaperman for the Singapore *Nippō*, the local Japanese-language newspaper, and shortly afterwards "M.6" told his police handlers of Kokubo's boasts. M.6 reported that Kokubo had bragged about paying large sums of money for secret documents from the Singapore RAF base, provided by a local Eurasian who claimed to have sources working on the base. According to the police, this was Percy Don, known as "D": a petty gangster and notorious con man, perpetrating his latest scam in a series of misleading claims that played on his self-proclaimed access to the installation. An investigation hardly seemed worthwhile: an unreliable undercover agent had provided the police with hearsay information about a drunken braggart's alleged espionage activities with a swindler who was more likely to "milk" the Japanese consulate of cash by empty promises or self-fabricated "secrets"[13] than provide useful intelligence (TNA, KV3/416, pp. 78–79).

Perhaps intending to impress "M.6," in early September the garrulous Kokubo described to him the Japanese intelligence network in Singapore and revealed that its communications link to Tokyo was Dr Ōuchi Tsune, a 46-year-old respected epidemiologist who had since 1929 served as the Deputy Director of the League of Nations Health Bureau in Singapore, a position that conferred diplomatic immunity. As Special Branch absorbed this startling new intelligence, "M.6" dropped another bombshell, telling his handlers that "D" claimed to have the RAF codebook, but that bargaining over a sale price with resident Japanese had been suspended pending the arrival of the motorized sailing vessel *Wani* maru. On September 14, Special Branch began watching various hotels, homes, and persons associated with Kokubo[14] (TNA, KV3/415, 60, 67–69).

Three days later the *Wani* maru visited Singapore on a voyage ostensibly intended to teach sailing skills to young Japanese Sea Scouts and promote international friendship during an extended journey through the South Seas. The disproportionate number of crewmembers (29) to scouts (28) seemed to confirm police suspicions that the visit was a cover for espionage, more so because according to police informants ten "research officers" were actually members of the Japanese navy's technical department[15] ("Brits in '34 feared Japan used Sea Scouts to mask espionage," Japan *Times*, 6 Mar 2006, 1; TNA, KV3/251, Serial 9 a., pp. 3–9). Several Sea Scout leaders participated in conferences on September 18 and attended a reception at the Japanese consulate in Singapore that included the Japanese naval attaché and prominent Japanese residents.

Only later did the British learn that scoutmaster Hara Michita and assistant master Adachi Shūzō, both retired Japanese navy captains, had slipped away from the main party to meet with Kokubo, Ohki, and Ōuchi. Kokubo told Hara that he could buy the codebook and other secret naval documents. He also said that Nishimura Yoshio, managing director in Singapore of *Ishihara sangyō kaiun kōshi* (Ishihara industrial and marine transport company) or ISK—the largest Japanese-owned industrial and mining concern in British Malaya—would pay for them with ISK money[16] (TNA, KV3/415, 73). Two undercover police informants separately reported the gist of the secret meeting. Although participants struck no deal, Hara and Adachi promised that "friends" would do so once the *Wani* maru departed Singapore[17] (TNA, KV3/415, 68).

ISK's participation in the conspiracy really mattered. Ishihara Hiroichirō, ISK's founder and owner, was the most prominent Japanese businessman in Southeast Asia before the Pacific War. During the 1920s and 1930s, he built his mining company, with Japanese government support, on the northwest Malayan peninsula. He opposed Western colonialism, encouraged nationalist movements, and, as a Japanese patriot, allowed his company to be used for espionage purposes (Peattie, 1996, pp. 202, 211; Tsu, n.d.). ISK had legitimate business and commercial reasons to collect openly available data on terrain, topography, and tropical conditions in the region, but its involvement in Japanese government-directed espionage made all of ISK's work suspect to British eyes and by extension cast a dark cloud of suspicion over the Japanese communities throughout Malaya as Anglo-Japanese tensions steadily increased during the post-First World War decades.

Although increasingly suspicious of what Kokubo was up to, local colonial officials were generally skeptical of the reports regarding Kokubo and disregarded their informants' accounts as exaggerations. The Inspector General of the Straits Settlement Police, Harold Fairburn, disapproved the Director of Special Branch's mid-October request to banish Kokubo from the colony[18]

(TNA, KV3/415, 72). Restraint seemed appropriate to the British civil authorities who, according to the security and military services, were personally adverse "to admitting the existence of espionage" and unwilling to fund counterespionage operations to protect a naval base that had been "imposed on them" from London and was therefore an imperial, not a local, commitment. For British residents, perhaps the naval base's only saving grace was that they did not have to pay for it. Instead, indirect taxes, paid largely by Singapore's Chinese-population, funded the annual defense subscription as well as special legislature-approved "gifts" for Imperial defense[19] (TNA, KV3/416, 3 & 73–74).

The colony had no security committee to provide counterintelligence guidance or coordinate counter-Japanese action. Each military service followed its respective doctrine. For direction, the civilian governor and senior police bureaucrats deferred to the Colonial Office in London, which was predisposed to counter communist subversion and not Japanese spying.

Police and military intelligence was not fully shared. For example, the Secret Intelligence Service's (SIS) Government Code and Cipher School (GCCS) solved the Japanese consular code early in 1934, and later that same year broke a machine cipher used by Japanese naval attachés. A cryptographic unit was established in Hong Kong harbor in April 1934, and two years later it evolved into the Far East Combined Bureau (FECB), the British cryptanalytic center in East Asia, which continued to exploit these sources to expose Japanese espionage in Malaya and elsewhere (Best, 2002, pp. 109–110, 124). But SIS did not distribute its signals intelligence to the police. Special Branch police relied on undercover work, much of it dependent on idiosyncratic or questionable agents, and had no official channel to pass on intelligence to the military. Rather, the police shared counterintelligence informally with the military as they saw fit and vice-versa, there being no established procedures for intelligence sharing among agencies until December 1939. In sum, and this is worth emphasizing, in the summer of 1934 no one knew precisely who was responsible for protecting the colony from foreign espionage.

At an August 1934 meeting at Government House between colonial and military officials, the naval representative argued that internal security was the Colonial Office's responsibility. Civilian authorities balked at the financial and personnel demands for additional police and linguists and recommended that the army shoulder the costs and provide the linguists[20] (TNA, KV3/415, 44, 50–51). According to Singapore's defense plan, however, the army and police were supposed to guard strategic locations to prevent sabotage and civil unrest, not operate a counterintelligence organization to identify possible enemy agents or spies. Although Special Branch had uncovered the Kokubo plot, combating anti-communist subversion remained its primary mission during the 1930s, even though the nascent conspiracy had exposed the widening extent of Japanese espionage and its accompanying security implications (Ban, 2001, p. 119). Without a common policy, as the naval member put it, no one "had thought out what action they would take if a spy was caught"[21] (TNA, KV3/415, 50–51,44, quote).

By early September, Kokubo was boasting about how much the Japanese would pay him for the codebook and for plans for the naval base and RAF installation. He became even more talkative as his anticipated payoff neared, and his carelessness exposed the entire plot and its participants to police informers. Between November 11 and 13, Kokubo implicated Nishimura not only as the ring's contact with Tokyo but also as its bagman and disclosed that Ōuchi told him that "a man from Kobe will come down to clinch the bargain." On the 19th Kokubo revealed that the man from Kobe would arrive on November 29, and four days later Ohki told "M.6" that the "man from Kobe" was a lieutenant commander in the imperial Japanese navy and that Nishimura was financing the final deal[22] (TNA, KV3/415, 70).

In less than two weeks, Kokubo had completely exposed the resident Japanese spy ring in Singapore, implicated two of the most prominent Japanese citizens in the colony, and compromised the Japanese Navy Ministry along with numerous hangers-on. Yet Singapore's senior civilian officials doubted that hearsay evidence alone was convincing enough for the Colonial Office to approve arrest warrants and so rejected Special Branch's request to detain two suspicious Japanese travelers upon their impending arrival in Singapore[23] (TNA, KV3/415, 36, 48). The day before the pair arrived, Special Branch police fortuitously intercepted and photographed a letter from a *Wani* maru crewmember to Kokubo which laid out the conspiracy, but without a Japanese translator it languished unread for six days[24] (TNA, KV3/415, 129, 48).

During the interlude, the two Japanese agents, as prearranged with Kokubo's spy ring, disembarked from the *Rio de Janeiro* maru using false names and fake passports provided by Japan's foreign ministry, with ISK supplying a business cover[25] for a

Kashima Teizō, the alias used by the undercover naval officer (TNA, KV3/415, 142). According to their travel documents, thirty-seven-year-old Kashima was an ISK employee in Singapore on business, and his younger companion, Kizaki Katsujirō, was a self-described writer. Passport control routinely stamped their papers and visas, admitting them to the colony. Nishimura greeted them wharf-side and took them to their respective hotels. Plainclothes Special Branch detectives shadowed the trio, aware from informers' tips that Kashima was actually a lieutenant commander in the Imperial Japanese Navy.

The Japanese spies initially registered on November 29 at separate Singapore hotels where they left their luggage, but Nishimura then took them to a third hotel in the suburbs: the Tokiwa Garden, a police-described "geisha house" by the seaside at Katong. They eventually stayed at the Tokiwa Garden and met with Kokubo several times, prodding him to produce the promised secret intelligence. Ohki and Nishimura also occasionally visited[26] (TNA, KV3/415, 129, 119, 60–61; KV3/416, 78–79). As Kashima and Kizaki grew openly skeptical about Kokubo's claims, he offered to bring "D" and the codebook to a December 1 meeting at his home. Kizaki, "D," and a third Japanese person allegedly from Siam attended[27] (TNA, KV3/415, 87, 70–71). During the bargaining, the Japanese soon realized that they were wasting their time because neither Kokubo nor "D" had any meaningful intelligence. The Siam operative vanished as quickly as he had appeared while the Kobe pair planned to return to Japan on December 3. Kokubo inveigled them to postpone their departure until the fifth by pleading that he needed just a few more days to get the plans for the naval base and installations.

"D" was sufficiently alarmed over the meeting that he reported in person to Special Branch Headquarters that day; this was the first time he had been to Headquarters since late September when police had warned him to stay away from Kokubo. "D" then corroborated "M.6" 's and Imaizumi's reports of the discussions[28] (TNA, KV3/415, 61, 95–96; KV3/415, 71).

Around the same time, the head of Singapore's Special Branch M. L. Wynne, frustrated by bureaucratic timidity, took matters into his own hands by pressuring one of his elderly Chinese informers to translate the previously intercepted letter from the *Wani* maru into Chinese. Wynne was a policeman trained in Mandarin and could possibly have translated the Chinese version into English. The circuitous translation outlined Tokyo's complicity in the espionage conducted by Kokubo and Ohki, and on this basis the colonial government finally authorized Special Branch to act against Kashima and Kizaki. The night of December 3 undercover police burgled the hotels where the Japanese spies had originally registered, stole Kizaki's passport, photographed it, and returned it. Kashima's passport was missing[29] (TNA, KV3/415, 36–37, 72, 48, 95, 61).

Special Branch knew from informants that Kashima and Kizaki planned to leave on December 5 and hurriedly cobbled together a sting operation to ensnare them and their accomplices. An RAF warrant officer approached Kokubo and offered to sell him secret documents, then agreed to bring the material to a meeting with Kashima and Kizaki for evaluation. The two spies had already given up on Kokubo and, sensing trouble, they instead sent Ohki as a cutout. Ohki naively offered to pay the RAF double agent for cipher keys as well as plans and photographs of the naval and air bases, thereby implicating himself and Kokubo, but not Kashima or Kizaki[30] (TNA, KV3/415, 62; KV3/416, 66–69).

Special Branch detectives arrested Kokubo and Ohki on December 5 for violation of the Official Secrets Act, and the Singaporean government authorized their banishment. Both were held at Singapore civil prison, pending Colonial Office concurrence. Kashima and Kizaki, however, had not incriminated themselves, so the police arrested and interrogated them on the night of December 4 going into 5 under Straits Settlement Ordinance 169. The ordinance permitted police to detain a person likely to encourage sedition or disrupt public order, or in possession of a false passport, for four days[31] (TNA, KV3/415, 53, 87, 62, 46).

In exchange for a guarantee that he and his assistant, whose true identity was never established, would be allowed to return to Japan, Kashima admitted that he was Lieutenant Commander Kaseda Tetsuhiko, assigned to the Naval General Staff's third department (Intelligence), seventh branch (European powers). Kaseda confessed that he had come to Singapore to obtain official secrets, and agreed to forfeit his luggage and be deported[32] (TNA, KV3/415, 48, 142). The police also demanded Kaseda's fake passport, which he told them Nishimura was holding for safekeeping. A police officer phoned Nishimura who dropped the passport off at the station that evening unaware that he too was deeply implicated in the spy ring[33] (TNA, KV3/415, 130, 49).

Special Branch kept its bargain and arbitrarily allowed Kaseda and Kizaki to return "quietly to Japan" without coordinating their release with the Services or the Colonial Office. Detectives escorted both spies aboard the *Kuruma* maru around 2:00 a.m. on December 5, though the vessel was not due to sail for another nine hours. Special Branch detectives did not allow the respective military representatives of Singapore to see Kaseda, but did inform the representatives of Kaseda's identity and the unilateral decision to allow both men to depart as scheduled on December 5[34] (TNA, KV3/415, 89, 119, 145, 142, 94).

Senior Singaporean police officials discreetly waited until after daybreak to inform the recently arrived Governor Straits Settlement Sir Shenton Thomas of the situation,[35] leaving him with the impression that the two spies had already set sail for Japan. No civilian authority thought to notify London. The resident naval officer unilaterally dispatched an unauthorized version of the incident to the British Admiralty and the British Commander-in-Chief, China. His December 5 cable was the first word of the arrests and deportations to reach London, where it provoked a prompt reaction that embarrassed Singapore's senior civil and police officials who vented their "seething indignation" on the naval officer[36] (TNA, KV3/415, 89, 119, 145, 142, 44).

As the investigation continued, the police determined that one of Kaseda's bags was missing. After a fruitless search of his hotel room, Wynne led detectives to the Tokiwa Garden. The hotel's proprietress stonewalled Wynne, vehemently denying that Kaseda had ever been there. Detectives ransacked the hotel until Wynne found Kaseda's camera, six thousand Malay dollars, and apparent cipher material concealed in the elaborate folds of the proprietress' kimono. Wynne later used the confiscated money to pay detectives "who would normally be employed on counter-communist activities for counter-Japanese purposes." This was, of course, a temporary expedient, but indicative of how Special

Branch's focus on communism drew personnel and resources from the counter-Japanese effort.

Wynne's detectives, however, could not account for a little bag that was suspected to contain secret naval plans. A Japanese prostitute had apparently removed this small leather attaché case from the Tokiwa Garden and passed it to an ISK employee who, in turn, in broad daylight and under the eyes of Special Branch detectives watching the pier, smuggled it to Kaseda already aboard the *Kuruma* maru awaiting departure. A chagrined Wynne admitted to the naval representative that one of his men "went to sleep on the job there"[37] (TNA, KV3/415, 96–97; KV3/416, 73, 91–92).

Subsequent police examination of Kaseda's confiscated luggage identified an engraved brass plate on a briefcase that commemorated the case as a gift to Kaseda Teizō from Lord William Francis Forbes-Semphill[38] (TNA, KV3/415, 96–97, 37, 49). For whatever reasons, Singapore's civil authorities kept this information to themselves. MI5 only learned of this latest twist in mid-December when the SIS informed it that a "reliable source" had reported a cable that acknowledged that Semphill knew Kaseda and had presented him with the bag. SIS suggested that Semphill might have additional background information regarding Kaseda[39] (TNA, KV3/415, 99). Lord Semphill's name raised eyebrows in MI5 since Japanese cables deciphered during the 1920s had revealed that he was passing classified information to Japan.

Semphill, then in Australia, was a British aviation pioneer who served as a pilot in the Royal Flying Corps and Royal Naval Air Service during the First World War. In 1922 he had led a British mission to Japan to promote Japanese naval aviation. Kaseda, as a lieutenant junior grade assigned to naval aviation, served as Semphill's escort officer in Tokyo that November and received the engraved briefcase as thanks. His close ties with Japanese naval colleagues and members of Tokyo's Foreign Ministry revived embarrassing questions about his loyalty. His lineage (his father was aide-de-camp to King George V) and his peerage shielded him from prosecution and left in place a spy for Japan who enjoyed access to the most rarified levels of British society and government. Sir Eric Holt-Wilson, the Deputy Director MI5, took personal charge of the matter and interviewed Semphill after his return from Australia about the Kaseda affair. In the event, it was determined that the gift was an innocent one. No further action was taken (Aurora, 2012, "Lord Semphill").

On December 6, the Chief Inspector, Special Branch M. P. Chand again summoned Nishimura from his well-to-do Oxley Rise home to answer questions about inconsistencies between the name engraved on the bag and the one on the passport. Minutes after entering the police station, Nishimura collapsed and died in a strychnine-induced suicide. Initial newspaper accounts tersely reported that Nishimura had dropped dead during police questioning and an autopsy was underway; an explanation that did not placate agitated Japanese residents who demanded answers from the police[40] (ST, December 6, 1934, p. 12 & ST, December 9, 1934, p. 1; *The Argus*, December 11, 1934, p. 9).

Rumors of suicide spread quickly and added to the shock of local Japanese communities because the late businessman also had been the president of Singapore's Japan Association (an umbrella organization for local Japanese groups) and a pillar of Japanese community[41] (*The Singapore Free Press and Mercantile Advertiser*,

December 7, 1934, p. 3). Japanese citizens would have been horrified to learn that Dr Ōuchi, the League of Nations' official and prominent resident who gave such delightful lectures on the tea ceremony, paid a resident Japanese prostitute the handsome sum of 40 Malay dollars (about $25 American) to retrieve Kaseda's bag from his hotel room following the spy's arrest[42] (TNA, KV3/426, 48).

Shenton Thomas downplayed the spy melodrama. The governor's December 8 summary to Colonial Office cited insufficient evidence to arrest Kaseda and his accomplice. If that was the case, replied the Secretary of State for the Colonies, why weren't the two detained for carrying false passports and admitting to espionage? Despite these questions, the same day, December 10, the secretary privately assured Shenton Thomas of London's support and reminded him that the home government desired minimum publicity about the incident to prevent an embarrassing parliamentary inquiry on the eve of scheduled Anglo-Japanese discussions on naval limitations[43] (TNA, KV3/415, 192–130, 132, 125).

Besides a lack of evidence, the official cover-up contended that an open trial would risk divulging state secrets, generating unwanted sensationalism, provoking official inquiries, or embarrassing Japan. Shenton Thomas consequently issued no official statement; he could not do so without mentioning Japan. Off-the-record, Shenton Thomas convinced Singapore newspaper editors to minimize reporting about the incident. The editors outdid themselves, omitting mention of Kaseda and Kizaki, the Singapore naval base, and the Japanese navy's involvement. Kokubo's and Ohki's arrests received only passing mention[44] (TNA, KV3/415, 132).

The death of an important and wealthy businessman in police custody was a sensational story that local papers could hardly ignore, but they did approach it discreetly. Nishimura's autopsy became the front-page story with hints of espionage that involved two recent but otherwise unidentified Japanese visitors and questions about the resident Japanese community's involvement in the "perplexing affair" (ST, "Allegations of Spying?," December 9, 1934, p. 1). For many Japanese people in Singapore, the sudden death of a community leader in police custody was another example of Anglo-Saxon discrimination and served only to heighten Japanese awareness of their fragile position in the colony, stir up anti-British and anti-colonial feelings, and generate greater sympathy for imperial Japan.

Deciphered cables exchanged among the Singapore consul-general, Bangkok, and Tokyo between December 5 and 8 enabled the British to piece together *ex post facto* the scope of the Japanese government's involvement in the conspiracy. A December 10 cable from the Singapore consul-general to the Foreign Ministry outlined the plot and the conspirators involved, naming Kokubo, Hara, Nishimura, Ohki, and Kaseda, and outlining the circumstances of Nishimura's suicide. Tokyo asked Singapore on December 18 if Kokubo and Ohki had already been deported. Singapore promptly replied that colonial authorities had yet to decide. On December 20, Singapore informed Calcutta that the spies had intended to purchase military documents from two Japanese residents[45] (TNA, KV3/415, 73).

Despite the Japanese espionage debacle in Singapore, Dr Ōuchi continued his clandestine activities shielded by diplomatic immunity. The doctor's official travels throughout the Malayan

Peninsula enabled him to routinely visit Japanese-owned mining, trading, and commercial concerns located there. He certainly received reports from the handful of Japanese long-term agents scattered among Japanese-owned commercial firms. These agents probably lived in the port cities and met with managers of Japanese-owned companies with mining or industrial interests in the north, and who gathered regional information for their respective commercial or industrial operations[46] (TNA, KV3/426, 92–93). Ōuchi, enjoying diplomatic immunity, likely couriered their reports back to the consulate for transmission to Tokyo, continuing his espionage role as the communications link between the Singapore consulate and the Japanese living and working in Malaya.

Ōuchi visited the small Japanese communities in towns along the coast or inland, which were administratively well-organized under the auspices of the Japan Association to promote common bonds of the Japanese language and culture among Japanese residents. Founded in 1915, the Japan Association was headquartered in Singapore, enjoyed close ties to the Japanese consulate, and through its locally organized chapters had become the largest public body governing the small Japanese communities (Yuen, 1978, pp. 172–173). Local chapters catered to the social needs of expatriates, promoted Japanese commerce, and emphasized Japan's uniqueness, which included the residents' ties to Japan. The chapters functioned administratively like a typical Japanese ward office (*kuyakusho*) and maintained records on every member of the community. The downside to such social cohesion was an aloof and self-contained community. The Japanese rarely interacted socially with the other Asian ethnic communities of Malay people, Indians, or Chinese people. Even in Singapore, social contact was usually limited to business dealings.

In the colonial setting, security police viewed the promotion of self-awareness and national identity as suspicious, if not outright subversive activities (Yuen, 1978, 176; Everest-Phillips, 2007, p. 246). These Japanese settlers were certainly sympathetic to Japan and likely anti-British, but they were not trained spies and Ōuchi never intended to recruit them for espionage. What would they spy on? No one, including Ōuchi, had any idea what might constitute an important target in Malaya because Tokyo had no war plans for the peninsula during the 1930s (Farrell, 2015, pp. 267–268).

Instead Ōuchi tapped into the ready-made social aspect of the Japan Association as the basis for an informal information (intelligence) gathering network of amateurs that he loosely coordinated through the Singapore consulate. Residents talked to him about what they saw or heard locally. Granted, much of this so-called intelligence was useless local gossip, but the institutional knowledge that Ōuchi accrued during the eight years spent in the colony and his frequent trips to the interior on official League of Nations Health Bureau business enabled him to evaluate the implications of external and internal changes to the local status quo. Such knowledge was useful during the colony's economic and commercial development boom of the later 1930s, but the information was openly available without having to resort to clandestine espionage.

London refused to compromise its intelligence sources by accusing Ōuchi of espionage, allowing the doctor to continue his clandestine activities without interruption. His official duties as an epidemiologist studying malaria control and prevention allowed him to travel freely throughout Malaya with official League sanction. He succeeded the late Nishimura as chairman of the Japan Association of Singapore, a position that encouraged contacts with all sorts of Japanese residents and visitors. Ōuchi remained untouchable, but the *Wani* maru did not.

In early 1935, the British naval attaché in Tokyo requested that the Japanese navy ministry clarify the status of four *Wani* maru crew members, ostensibly in order to accord them the proper official precedence that their military ranks entitled them to in future visits[47] (JCAR Ref. No. C11080567900). The not-so-subtle query included the names and civilian titles of three retired navy captains who were the ship's commander, the leader of the Tokyo Sea Scouts (Adachi), and the head of the Sea Scouts (Hara), respectively, as well as the navy lieutenant junior grade technician assigned to the navy's technical institute. The formal inquiry produced a flurry of official correspondence within the navy and foreign ministries about the *Wani* maru's status, and shortly thereafter the navy prohibited both active duty and reserve naval officers like Hara or Adachi from participating in Sea Scout programs[48] (JCAR Ref. No. B04012431900; Ennyū, 2005, pp. 41–54).

Kaseda's naval career was in tatters. He was reassigned from the naval general staff to the far less prestigious staff of the Yokosuka Navy Yard in February 1935. That October, the navy promoted him to full commander, but just two months later relieved him from duty and placed him on the inactive list because of his involvement in a tiny religious sect that was disbanded by the government for *lèse majesté*.[49] According to a Dutch propaganda report, Kaseda reemerged in the Netherlands East Indies in 1940 using an alias but still working for Ishihara *sangyō* (NEIG, 1942, p. 128). This seems dubious given that Kaseda was tried for *lèse majesté* in February 1941 and received a three-year suspended sentence. He was re-arrested in early 1944, survived the war, and died in 1971.

2
Under suspicion

Regardless of the multiple humiliations Kokubo had wrought, Japan's Singapore consulate remained the centerpiece of the Japanese intelligence effort in Malaya throughout the 1930s. The consulate staff overtly and covertly gathered political and diplomatic intelligence, linked the navy's and the foreign ministry's intelligence collection efforts, provided either diplomatic cover or phony documents for agents, served as a clearinghouse for operatives' reports, and acted as a communications center by sending intelligence to Tokyo in enciphered diplomatic cables or via diplomatic pouches[50] (TNA, KV3/426, 91–92). Lastly, the consulate provided contacts that the spies could tap into among Japanese expatriates residing in British Malaya's communities as well as disaffected indigenous groups, some funded by the consulate.

Alarm over the Kaseda spy ring and Singapore's "apparently rather weak action" convinced "K" (Sir Vernon Kell, the director of MI5) that "a separate continuous service Security Officer" was needed in Singapore; this view was shared by the Colonial Office, which offered to defray the security officer's salary[51] (TNA, KV3/416, 3). Singapore's civil authorities also requested additional personnel and money to allow the security police to counteract the Japanese danger to the colony. Neither the money nor the personnel were forthcoming because of the demands of the "communist threat." Instead, Singapore's bureaucrats reorganized the police. Fairburn retired in early 1935 and was replaced by Rene Onraet as Inspector General of Police. Onraet's reputation rested on his energetic anti-communist record, but as Special Branch Director in Singapore he had backed counter-Japanese operations. MI5 expected that he would provide better support than Fairborn who had displayed little interest in counterespionage work. Onraet and Wynne seemed like the ideal combination to root out Japanese espionage, but they disliked each other, which led Wynne to resign as head of Special Branch, Singapore[52] (TNA, KV3/416, 72 and 74).

Special Branch, organized in the 1920s to ferret out communists, had established a Japanese section in 1934. Indian Army Major Kenneth Morgan (retired), the head of the Japanese Section, was considered by then Colonel A. E. Percival (who would later command British ground troops during the Malayan campaign and surrender Singapore to the Japanese in February1942), an eccentric who lacked judgment and common sense (Coxy, 2009, Post No. 3).

Morgan was a Japanese speaker who amassed voluminous intelligence files (every Japanese fisherman had to have a separate card) on the Japanese in Malaya, which he refused to share with Special Branch, the military, or colonial officials. His unwillingness to cooperate with higher authorities and his tendency to tell them only what he wanted them to know while pressing his oft-times outrageous views on them made it easy to dismiss him as a "scaremonger"[53] (CUDL, Civilian Internment, pp. 34–41, 55). His eccentricities were another source of amusement. For example, ignoring Singapore's heat, Morgan always wore a sleeveless woolen pullover and refused to turn on the fan in the tiny office that he shared with his secretary. His growing paranoia convinced him that he was the target of imminent assassination, and consequently Morgan and his secretary led what she described as "a sort of cloak and dagger life." He also had a disconcerting habit of falling asleep in mid-sentence, something he once did while interrogating a suspected Japanese spy. Nonetheless his secretary greatly admired him and remembered Morgan as the "kindest & most forbearing of all her bosses"[54] (CUDL, Civilian Internment, pp. 49–51).

Morgan also refused to talk to the extremely aggressive MI5 Defense Security Officer (DSO) F. Hayley Bell, newly appointed in 1936 and described as "a deaf madman" by the deputy head of MI5. Bell at least had an excuse for his attitude. He had twice been seriously wounded on the Western Front during the First World War and had suffered a fearful beating to the head during a 1930 dockworkers' strike in Hong Kong. Morgan regarded Bell, who was in charge of security and counterintelligence in Singapore, as a security risk and refused to share information with him about Japanese espionage[55] (Walton, 2013, pp. 22–23; Best, 2002, p. 152; Peter, 2009, Post No. 1). That British colonial bureaucrats and London tolerated the conduct of the pair suggests that such odd behavior was expected in sensitive clandestine overseas posts. Perhaps indicative of the colonial mindset, a British contemporary attributed their idiocrasies to the "Chinese madness:" an affliction of those "who studied and learnt Chinese"[56] (CUDL, Civilian Internment, p. 31).

If Morgan was secretive, Bell was flamboyant. As if to demonstrate his zeal for counterespionage, one of Bell's early reports to

London described him crawling through a drainage tunnel to determine if a saboteur carrying explosives could infiltrate the naval base through the drains. In order to neutralize Japanese espionage, Bell engaged in schemes of dubious legality. He recruited volunteers to penetrate the Japanese spy network. His counterspies reported uncovering a Japanese plan to land an invasion force in Thailand and northern Malaya and then move south against Singapore (Thompson, 2005, pp. 40–41). When Shenton Thomas dismissed the report out of hand (indeed, at the time the Japanese had no such intentions), Bell stubbornly clung to the idea. Besides repeatedly pressing this opinion on the increasingly exasperated Governor General, Bell's booming voice publicly denounced Shenton Thomas's incompetence to all who cared to listen.

Bell also reported in April 1937 that the Japanese were "systematically sounding the approaches to the Naval Base," conjuring up stereotypes from the 1920s when rumors abounded that undercover Japanese naval officers crewed fishing boats[57] (TNA, KV3/251 Serial 9 a., 1; Best, 2002, p, 103). With some justification, both Bell and Morgan resurrected similar suspicions that the current fishing fleet carried Japanese naval officers masquerading as lowly fishermen.

Eifuku Tora, a Japanese resident of Singapore, owned the largest and wealthiest fishing operation in Singapore. He was typical of pan-Asianist Japanese businessmen of the era. He was a vocal critic of Britain's economic policies, which banned his fleets from fishing grounds off the Solomon Islands and Burma and set increasingly restrictive licensing requirements that put about 600 of 1,500 Japanese fishermen, comprising the majority of

Japanese residents of Singapore, out of business between 1937 and 1939 (History, 2014). He likely did allow naval personnel on his fishing trawlers during the 1930s as Bell and Morgan suspected and definitely did so during 1940 and 1941.

The outbreak of the Sino-Japanese War in July 1937 caused a crackdown of sorts on suspected Japanese agents in Singapore. In late December 1937, Shenton Thomas requested the Colonial Office's permission to expel five suspected Japanese spies from Singapore, including Goma Shohei (an alias) and Tsujimori Tanizō, a South Seas specialist and author of several well-received books about Malaya and the Netherlands East Indies. Goma was a professional spy who the British believed was organizing a Muslim spy network in Singapore. Tsujimori, however, seemed tainted by allegations that he was simultaneously colluding with two irreconcilable groups: the reactionary Japanese Black Dragon Society and the revolutionary Sumatran communists. All five suspects were banished without fanfare in February 1938 (Best, 2002, pp.152–153; Elphick and Smith M., 1994, pp. 146–147; Kennard, 1947, p. 6).

Even further behind the scenes, at Special Branch's request, the governor added Dr Ōuchi's name to the banishment list because of his close ties to "the Japanese espionage system in Singapore" and noted that only diplomatic immunity had kept Ōuchi off the original list[58] (TNA, CO273/644/9). Informal Foreign Office discussions about Ōuchi's status with League representatives in Geneva in early 1938 ended inconclusively because the League required *prima facie* evidence of his misconduct, which the British government refused to divulge[59] (TNA, CO273/644/9). Singapore authorities next pressured Ōuchi by intimating to the Japanese consul-general that London would act officially against the doctor unless he left the colony. But after a decade in Singapore, Ōuchi was too "well entrenched" for such a ploy and the Colonial Office apparently was unwilling to take on "a laborious business to dig him out"[60] (TNA, CO273/644/9). Ōuchi eluded British authorities and continued to use his position in the cause of Japanese espionage until sometime in 1941 when he moved to Shanghai.

With Ōuchi out of play, Morgan's biggest catch was Goma Shohei, reputedly a mastermind of Japanese espionage in Singapore and regarded as a dangerous man. In late 1937, Morgan took personal charge of Goma's interrogation and, accompanied by his private secretary Barbara Brown, interviewed Goma in a tiny examination room at Pearl's Hill Gaol. Morgan and Goma sat facing each other across a narrow table while Brown sat at the end taking notes. Morgan questioned Goma in Japanese and passed the dialogue in English to the note-taking secretary. In the middle of one question, Morgan suddenly fell asleep. Goma and Brown looked at each other, one hardly believing his luck, the other too well aware of her danger. Brown recovered in time to kick Morgan's leg under the table. Startled awake, Morgan continued the session as if nothing unusual had happened. When the interrogation was complete, Morgan and Brown returned to Special Branch and gaolers returned Goma to his cell to await deportation[61] (CUDL, Civilian Internment, pp. 50–52).

Japan's undeclared war with China triggered widespread Chinese boycotts of Japanese goods. The Japanese business community in Singapore was especially vulnerable because Japanese merchants relied on a network of Chinese compradors to distribute their products to the Chinese community (Peattie, 1996, p. 200; Koh and Tanaka, 1984, p. 392). Indian residents of Singapore had established businesses, and some saw the boycott as an opportunity to open new branches to expand their share in the lucrative transfer of Japanese-produced goods. Even if they managed to sidestep the tight Chinese control of distribution, however, they lacked the know-how to disburse the exports, overextended themselves, and were forced out of business.

Tokyo quickly recognized the serious economic repercussions of the Chinese boycott on Singapore's Japanese merchant community and launched countermeasures. By late spring 1938, the Singapore Consul General and the recently arrived correspondent for *Dōmei* (Japan's official news agency) Kobayashi Ishirō were organizing a propaganda campaign to discredit Chiang K'ai-shek, the leader of Nationalist China. But the boycott intensified month after month, leaving resident Japanese merchants in "a stage of exhaustion and difficulty"[62] (TNA, KV3/252, 27–28, 31). At the Singapore consulate's urging and with Tokyo's encouragement, two large Japanese banks provided low-interest loans to Japanese merchants to repay debts owed to Chinese compradors. The consulate was simultaneously and secretly subsidizing the Singapore *Nippō* to publish pro-Japanese and anti-Chiang propaganda in its Chinese newspaper and its English-language edition the Singapore *Herald*[63] (TNA, KV3/252, 42). The propaganda campaign backfired. By November 1938, anti-Japanese sentiment had spread among British merchants and, as the Japanese saw it, the local Singapore authorities not only refused to act against the boycott but also appeared to encourage it[64] (TNA, KV3/252, 3334, 38; Koh and Tanaka, 1984, p. 394).

Routine reports from police informants heightened Morgan's obsessions about the Japanese danger in Singapore. He concluded that should a successful anti-boycott campaign intimidate the Chinese community it would "jeopardize the future of Malaya"[65] (TNA, KV3/252, 50). He continually updated his card files; tracked Japanese visitors to Singapore; watched prominent Japanese figures such as Ohara Tomoyoshi, a senior official in Singapore's Japan Industrial Bureau; and kept tabs on transiting Japanese ships, being convinced that they carried secret agents from ultranationalist Japanese organizations and "possibly officers in mufti"[66] (TNA, KV3/252, 55). Aware of Ohara's involvement in the propaganda campaign and learning that Ohara was soon to return to Japan, Morgan decided to seize "documentary evidence" of Japanese treachery and presumably prevent Ohara's departure[67] (TNA, KV3/252, 51).

Having made up his mind, Morgan launched his January 18, 1939, night raids, acting under the Official Secrets Act but failing to inform higher authorities either in Singapore or London. Special Branch Police cordoned off the *Chūō dōri* neighborhood for several hours while Morgan's two- or three-man teams raided four targets, including Eifuku Tora's home, a Japanese-run hotel where three South Manchurian Railway (SMR) employees were staying, and the Japan Trade Bureau that shared office space with the South Seas Association (SSA)[68] (TNA, KV3/252, 14).

The SSA was a Japanese quasi-government organization established with foreign ministry backing in Tokyo in 1914, whose Singapore office dated to 1916. The SSA's published charter was to gather publicly available information and train young Japanese in order to facilitate economic penetration of Southeast Asia and elsewhere in the "South Seas." Branches spread to Malaya's commercial ports and business centers, where members originally collected openly available economic data. As a fixture in Japanese communities across Malaya, the SSA provided convenient cover for operatives from Japanese civilian ministries sent on specific intelligence missions and by the late 1930s it would become a valuable intelligence source for Japan's military planners (Peattie, 1996, pp. 198–199, 226).

Overall, Morgan's raids produced disappointing results. Police found nothing incriminating at Eifuku's residence. The three SMR employees had a restricted railway instruction manual which they claimed they got from "someone" in the Singapore consulate[69] (TNA, KV3/252, 51–52). They were not arrested but the authorities did deport all three two days later. Furthermore, although the police confiscated no hard evidence incriminating the SSA, guilt-by-association did increase regional suspicions of the SSA's role and gave rise to a "tentative theory" in British and Dutch intelligence services that the SSA was a widespread cadre capable of spreading Japanese propaganda or gathering intelligence for Tokyo[70] (TNA, KV3/252, 5–6). The extent of SSA espionage remained unknown, but its colony-wide network seemed ideal for intelligence collection, making it suspicious and therefore a police target.

Morgan personally led the raid on the Japan Trade Bureau, which uncovered a dozen aerial photos of Singapore and a series of letters and cables from Ohara to Tokyo dealing with ways to implement and fund measures to counter the Chinese boycott.

During the search, the Japanese vice-consul arrived to protest the raid and worsening anti-Japanese oppression. Morgan brushed him aside and, brandishing the aerial photos, suggested there was no need to involve the press[71] (TNA, KV252/3, 15–17). Two days later, The *Straits Times* published such a cursory account of the raids as to be meaningless ("Police Seize Documents," ST, January 21, 1939, p. 12; Kennard, 1947, p. 6). Morgan prepared his histrionic after-action accounts and promptly filed them, leaving Singapore authorities and MI5 mystified about what had happened. The raids produced scant intelligence, no arrests, and considerable embarrassment for British authorities who were at a loss to explain them.

In early March, Morgan apparently again overstepped his bounds when Special Branch police questioned a Japanese national traveling on a diplomatic passport before allowing him to enter Singapore. Special Branch police investigators later summoned the visitor to headquarters for further cross-examination. Tokyo protested this breach of diplomatic protocol and also denounced British provocateurs, possibly agents on Bell's MI5 payroll, who tried to entrap prominent local Japanese by surreptitiously offering them blueprints, photographs, and drawings of Singapore's defense works[72] (ST, March 2, 1939, p. 13). At a time when British authorities were trying to avoid a confrontation with Japan, it seemed that the Japan Section of Singapore's Special Branch and the local MI5 office were unilaterally ratcheting up hard feelings.

On March 4, the Director of MI5 had instructed T. A. Robertson of MI5 Intelligence to follow up on an earlier query to DSO Bell to question the police further on the January raids, of which MI5 still had "heard nothing"[73] (TNA, KV3/252, 11). Bell had concurrently taken over Special Branch, coincidentally on the morning following Morgan's overnight raids. On March 24, he forwarded Morgan's lengthy reports of the raids to the Director, MI5, Sir Vernon Kell, along with an apology attributing his delay to an oversight[74] (TNA, KV252/3, 12). In reality, this may have been the first time Bell ever saw the files given Morgan's antipathy toward him. Morgan's private secretary had left the Japan Section on January 30 to be married, leaving the precious files under new control. Morgan also soon departed, placed on extended leave perhaps because of the diplomatic repercussions of his raids and the ensuing diplomatic protests. Without Morgan or his secretary guarding the files, Bell finally gained unfettered access to them[75] (CUDL, Civilian Internment, pp. 49–50).

But Bell too overstepped his bounds. His questionable methods, such as creating a vigilante cadre, alleged condoning of summary executions, and, worst of all, loudly (literally) criticizing the governor-general's policies in public, led to his dismissal in May 1939 (Peter, 2009, Post No. 1). Around the same time, Morgan was also officially replaced as Special Branch's Japanese section head by Alan E.C. Blades, a Straits Settlement Special Branch officer selected in 1936 for a three-year intensive Japanese-language training program in Japan. The damage, however, was done. Morgan's and Bell's antics and idiosyncrasies, their mutual hostility, and their unsubstantiated assertions of an imminent Japanese danger to the colony convinced Singapore's military establishment that Special Branch's intelligence was worthless.

Relations between the Special Branch police and the military never recovered from the poisonous relationship between Bell and

Morgan. Right up to the eve of the Japanese invasion, the military services paid little heed to security police reports or dismissed them for "lacking credence"[76] (TNA, KV3/426, 72). Intelligence cooperation between Special Branch and the Services virtually collapsed. Two experienced Special Branch agents wrote with dry understatement that cooperation "might, we are inclined to feel, have been considerably closer, with advantage to all concerned"[77] (TNA, KV3/426, 81). The propensity of military officers to talk openly in public—in clubs, cafes, and bars—about classified military matters incensed the police who felt that they did all the dirty work to gather valuable intelligence while the services "sit back and fail to keep their house in order"[78] (TNA, KV3/426, 105).

Spy-hunting detectives, undercover agents, agent provocateurs, and paid informers worked the sleazy underside of the Japanese community. Daily involvement with suspected spies, double agents, dope dealers, smugglers, and petty criminals convinced Special Branch that it needed broader powers to round up Japanese in places they deemed suspicious, to detain and inter Japanese residents, to expel the Japanese en masse from the colony, or to shut down the Singapore consulate. Each request for such sweeping authority met the same reply from London: comply with the law that entitled Japanese residents to the same treatment as other aliens in the colony and that made mass deportations or internments legally impermissible and discriminatory. What to do with the Japanese residents of Malaya remained contentious until the outbreak of war[79] (TNA, KV3/426, 111 and 118).

Of course, not all Japanese businessmen in Singapore were spies, but Japanese agents had their effectiveness multiplied by a sympathetic Japanese expatriate community in British Malaya.

Japanese operatives, using business covers, blended seamlessly into the tightly connected ethnic community and exploited a small core network of part-time informants, ranging from pimps to pillars of the community, to collect information from the larger population. There were a very few long-term agents like Ōuchi or paymasters like Nishimura in place; more part-time paid informants like Okubo, or petty criminals, or entertainers; and many more informers (witting or unwitting sources of information) whose allegiances were to Japan, but whose actions did not extend to espionage.

Special Branch's 1937 annual report acknowledged that three years of Morgan's Japanese subsection had increased counter-espionage efforts "though this work is hardly out of its initial state" (Ban, 2001, p. 165). Morgan's spreading paranoia conjectured a widespread Japanese spy network in Singapore. The lack of evidence to support his claims only "proved" that the Japanese spies were too clever to leave traces of their espionage. As for Bell, his reports to London told of Japanese saboteurs, of naval officers aboard commercial ships spying on Singapore, of ships transmitting secret messages to Tokyo, and of Japan's plans to invade Malaya. His vehement insistence throughout his tenure that Japanese spies were aiding the Japanese military's plans to capture Singapore from the north via Malaya skewed his relations with Governor General Shenton Thomas and ultimately led to his relief. In practical terms, Morgan and Bell accomplished little, but they did revive the shopworn Japanese bogeyman of the 1920s and put all of Singapore's Japanese under suspicion.

3

Tokyo reconsiders a Singapore strategy

Singapore had been center stage for Japanese spy—British counter-spy drama because the underdeveloped Malayan peninsula had no military installations of interest. By the mid-1930s, however, a spate of road and railway construction throughout Malaya had stimulated economic development and opened macadam and asphalt paved roads, expanded railways, and improved ports along the peninsula's west coast. The peninsula's western side could support heavy commercial and military traffic, making an overland attack on Singapore from the north feasible (Farrell, 2015, p. 92; Allen, 1991, pp. 44–45; Yamamoto, 2016, pp. 207–208). Malaya Command recognized this new risk and in 1937 called for ground troops and aircraft to defend the entire peninsula. Unwilling to commit large numbers of ground troops, the British Chiefs of Staff instead promised substantial aerial reinforcements. The Royal Air Force (RAF) promptly began an airfield construction program but did not coordinate the airfields' locations with the army. As a consequence, many of the 27 airstrips completed by the end of 1941 were poorly sited in vulnerable locations, isolated, and difficult to defend against ground attack. Promises to meet aircraft requirements—RAF Far East estimated 582 aircraft; the British Chiefs of Staff 336—fell by the wayside, usually justified with the rationalization that Japanese air power was overrated. When the Japanese blow fell the British had only 158 aircraft available and most were obsolete (Probert, 1995, p. 10; Farrell, 2015, pp. 93–96; Kennedy, 2010, p. 772; Allen, 1991, pp. 50–52).

Worsening Anglo-Japanese relations and the expanding Singapore naval base caused Japanese strategists to designate Great Britain a hypothetical enemy for the first time in their June 1936 revision of Imperial Defense Policy. This precaution, as the respective chiefs of staff explained to the emperor, was occasioned by the quickening reinforcement of the Hong Kong and Singapore bases and the threatening international situation (Yamamoto, 2016, p. 153). Revised imperial defense policy required the respective services to prepare operational contingency plans against Britain. The original versions drafted in August 1936 were rudimentary and the outbreak of the China war in July 1937 delayed the second iteration.

Japan's undeclared war in China hastened the transformation of Singapore's naval base. Thousands attended ceremonies marking the completion of the King George VI dry dock in mid-February, 1938. At 1,000 feet long by 130 feet wide and 35 feet deep, its massive size could accommodate the largest capital ships of the day. The occasion also served as the official opening of the enlarged naval base. That December, Japanese naval intelligence reported approximately 6,000 ground troops in Malaya, about one-third of them Indian soldiers; one aircraft carrier and three heavy cruisers, plus supporting warships in Asian waters; and 24 torpedo planes and 12 flying boats assigned to Singapore. Japanese naval intelligence analysts estimated that another 400 aircraft from British bases in Africa, the Middle East, and India could reinforce Singapore[80] (JCAR Ref. Nos. C1412185500 and C14121185800).

Earlier that year, Imoto Kumao, a 35-year-old captain assigned to the Army General Staff's (AGS) operations branch, and his navy counterpart prepared an operational plan that for the first time identified Singapore as a major ground objective. Building on Imoto's work, in February 1939 army planners proposed an invasion via Siam followed by a 500-mile offensive thrust along Malaya's west coast, culminating in the capture of Singapore (Yamamoto, 2016, pp. 74, 176–180). Most operations branch officers, being involved in fighting a war in China and planning for one against the Soviet Union, rejected the desktop plan. They stereotyped Malaya as an underdeveloped wilderness whose equatorial climate, impassable jungles, and patchwork road and rail networks suited wild animals and uncivilized natives but not military operations. Pending a staff officer's eyewitness assessment, branch officers refused to make any decision. Overseas espionage was ordinarily an intelligence function, but the AGS regarded intelligence officers as second-raters and furthermore lacked confidence in the Singapore consulate's ability to assess the military specifics required by army staff planners. Instead, the AGS their own recently promoted Major Imoto to Malaya for an on-the-ground appreciation of the feasibility of his draft plan (Yamamoto, 2016, p. 196).

Imoto originally intended to go as an "illegal" using false papers, but the potential international repercussions of being arrested by British authorities as a spy caused him to reconsider. He applied for and received visas to travel to British Malaya and other European colonies in Southeast Asia, ostensibly to liaise with Japanese military attachés and consulates (Yamamoto, 2016, pp. 186–187). In mid-August 1939, he arrived in French Indochina and reconnoitered road and rail networks, airfields, and possible sites for airfield construction. Next, he investigated potential landing beaches in southern Siam (Thailand) and on September 8 set off for Singapore. By that time Europe was at war and Britain was fighting Germany, Japan's ally. Nevertheless, British civilian and military officials treated Imoto cordially and with professional courtesy when he crossed the Siam border into Malaya.

Imoto spoke no English, but the Singapore consulate and the established Japanese trading companies like ISK, Mitsui, and Mitsubishi, to name a few, provided him with assistants, drivers, interpreters, local guides, and entry into the resident Japanese communities. He stayed at small Japanese inns and spent considerable time talking to the local Japanese residents, all the while reconnoitering key landing beaches and installations along Malaya's west coast. He was also lucky. By the time of his mission, Tokyo had switched to new enciphering systems that prevented prying British cryptanalysts from reading Japanese diplomatic and naval message traffic (Best, 2002, p. 138). The January 1938 changes to Japan's naval ciphers rendered them unreadable to cryptanalysts. The following February, the introduction of a new machine enciphering system denied the British (and Americans) access to Japanese Foreign Ministry communications.

Although the special intelligence blackout left British authorities unsure about Imoto's exact purpose in Malaya, they were certain that he was up to no good. Special Branch detectives conspicuously tailed him, once confiscating a map of Malaya that he had brought from Tokyo. For his part, Imoto committed nothing to paper and took no photographs. Instead, he memorized what he saw and later prepared his secret reports secure in the Singapore consulate.

A *Dōmei* newspaper reporter, likely Kobayashi Ishirō who had arrived the previous year, accompanied Imoto partway down the coast and provided much useful intelligence about the improved coastal defenses, minefields, and so forth. Imoto reached Singapore on September 11 where he told British authorities that he was travelling on "long leave," a sabbatical traditionally granted to Japanese staff officers. Posing as a tourist, he surveyed Singapore's northern defenses, and when British officers entertained him at Fort Canning, he took advantage of the fort's sweeping views of Singapore city and its waterfront to study the defensive works. He talked to local Japanese businessmen and later reconnoitered the Mersing beaches on the east coast, ruling them unsuitable as landing areas for large units because the rough waves might swamp landing craft and the thick jungle growth would severely restrict beachhead egress[81] (Yamamoto, 2016, pp. 187–192).

What Imoto saw firsthand surprised him. Instead of impassible jungle teeming with wild animals, he found all-weather paved roads that extended the length of Malaya's west coast. He traveled on rail lines that connected inland sites to coastal ports. He stopped in small commercial cities and ports and many smaller towns. In short, he saw a line of communication infrastructure capable of supporting large unit operations throughout Malaya. He also recognized British military weakness exemplified by the presence of a single British infantry battalion garrisoning the entire Malaya peninsula. Imoto returned to Tokyo convinced that his plan could work. His report and first-hand observations persuaded influential AGS staff officers that it might indeed be possible to capture Singapore overland from the north. More reconnaissance probes were needed to be sure, but the imperial army committed to additional detailed intelligence gathering throughout the Malay Peninsula.

Singapore's naval base remained the priority for Japanese consular agents who found themselves operating under more restrictive British wartime security measures following the outbreak of war in Europe. In response to changing British counterintelligence tactics, the Japanese improved their intelligence gathering capability in neighboring Thailand (formerly Siam), whose leaders appeared sympathetic, or at least not overtly hostile, to Japan. In August 1939, Colonel Tamura Hiroshi arrived in Bangkok to serve as the new military attaché at the Japanese consulate. Tamura was a seasoned intelligence agent, having spied on American military installations on Corregidor, Philippines, for three years (1928–1931) while posing as a laundry manager. He revitalized the Bangkok legation, which under his direction became the hub for Japanese espionage operations in Southeast Asia, Singapore having outlived its usefulness because of new wartime restrictions introduced on Japanese nationals (Reynolds, 1994, pp. 30–31, 34–35; Best, 2002, p. 153; Hata (ed.), 1991, p. 86). Imoto's report to the AGS and Tamura's posting to Bangkok not only shifted the emphasis of Japanese military espionage geographically northward but also made clear that the imperial army had taken charge.

Despite its relegation to a lesser supporting status, the Singapore consulate continued to use consular officials, paid agents, and sympathetic Japanese residents to collect intelligence and to foment a subversion campaign among the Malay residents of Singapore. Tokyo made no apparent effort through November, 1941, to coordinate these military and diplomatic subversion initiatives. Japanese spies attached to or directed by the consulate still remained active in Singapore. Three days after the outbreak of the European war, Japanese naval intelligence reported that "work on [Singapore] base proceeding faster than projected with two docks nearing construction. With exception of coastal battery on east side of waterway, outer works mostly completed and the gradual increase in air power is continuing"[82] (JCAR Ref. No. C14121193200). The analysis, probably based on the naval attaché's firsthand observations, was more sophisticated than the earlier reports from the 1930s that simply recounted newspaper articles or published official notices.

Repercussions from the distant war in Western Europe added to the counterintelligence burden in Malaya. British officials had to account for about 100 German nationals who were enemy aliens, as well as Italian nationals who were not but soon might be, and of course the resident Japanese. Special Branch retrospectively complained that even after the outbreak of war in September, 1939, London's legal restrictions permitted, "far too much freedom of movement" to aliens in Singapore and endorsed the security services' recommendations for stricter control of the Japanese. London insisted that Japanese residents were entitled to the same treatment as other aliens and that discriminatory action would have repercussions for British national security and interests in Japan. This course of action led the Singapore DSO. to comment in late March, 1941, that "A more 'forward' policy would enhance security all around." It is worth stating that eight months later Singapore's Defence Security Committee was still debating proper measures to restrict the activities and personal freedom of all Japanese residents[83] (TNA, KV3/426, 99, 118, 107). In the summer of 1939, however, other actions were underway in Singapore to offset continuing Japanese aggression.

In August 1939, London transferred the FECB from Hong Kong to Singapore because the Japanese army's occupation of nearby Guangzhou (Canton) placed the decryption center in jeopardy. That December, FECB established a new counterespionage section: the Far East Security Service (FESS), which served as a clearinghouse, pooling all-source intelligence to keep track of Japanese movements (Best, 2002, pp. 155–156). To combat the accelerated Japanese agitation of Indians and Malays, in early 1940 Special Branch created a Counter Japanese Encroachment Unit within the existing Japanese Section. Despite its impressive title, the unit lacked sufficient manpower and funding to deal effectively with the expanding Japanese subversion menace (Bridges, 1986, p. 25; Ban, 2001, p. 215). Furthermore, coordination and dissemination of sensitive material remained haphazard; a hangover from the Morgan-Bell controversies. Special Branch's "black list," a compilation of more than one-hundred suspected subversives, was highly classified and restricted to British headquarters and commanding officers. They pronounced it "of little use" and argued that without definite disciplinary measures officers could not prevent fraternization between their troops and the alleged Japanese spies[84] (TNA, KV3/426, 99). Colonial

Office authorities and local officials consistently rejected police attempts to restrict contact between Japanese shopkeepers and British soldiers and sailors because they risked the British Government "laying itself open to a charge of discrimination against a friendly (?) power"[85] (TNA, KV3/426, 123). The "friendly power" was becoming less friendly with each passing day.

The governing colonial authorities and Special Branch police were always vigilant for any evidence of civil discontent, particularly anti-colonial and anti-British attitudes, among the ruled indigenous populations. This was especially the case for Chinese communists, but also included the resident Japanese. Malaya Command viewed the expatriate Japanese communities as essentially a fifth column, spreading anti-British propaganda and plotting an uprising to betray Malaya from within. The Command distinguished, however, between aggressive spying (espionage) and passive collection (intelligence) to conclude in April 1940 that "No elaborate espionage organisations are believed to exist but it is known that the Japanese have well developed Intelligence Organisations throughout the country"[86] (TNA, KV3/426, 125). In fact, by that time there were both, and the rapidly changing international situation was shifting Singapore's emphasis to espionage.

Tokyo regarded Nazi Germany's stunning military victories in France and the Low Countries during May and June 1940 as a once-in-a-lifetime chance to act against the isolated European colonies in Asia. The Imperial General Headquarters' confidential diary recorded an enthusiasm for a southern advance that marked a 180-degree turn in the Army's thinking. The Army General Staff, for the first time, seriously considered Imoto's recommendations.

The AGS operations division disclosed its southern strategy with a Singapore scenario at a June 22, 1940, planning conference. The Senior War Ministry and AGS staff officers were caught off-guard because, as far as they knew, such a plan was operationally unsound if not downright reckless[87] (Tanemura (ed.), 1979, pp. 33, 36).

Most staff officers knew relatively little about Southeast Asia compared to the decades' worth of data available at their fingertips about projected battlefields in northern Manchuria or the Soviet Union (Hata et al. (eds.), 1963, p. 177). Lieutenant Colonel Yahara Hiromichi, an American specialist in the AGS intelligence department, expressed the dismissive conventional wisdom that the southern area was a "half-civilized barbaric region swarming with elephants and poisonous snakes" (Reynolds, 1994, p. 21). Senior army planners demanded more detailed intelligence before committing to a southern operation, and that June the AGS dispatched a handful of select mid-level operations branch staff officers to Southeast Asia and the Philippines to gather intelligence in the projected areas of operations. Depending upon their destinations, some in the first contingent traveled openly on legitimate visas or as "diplomatic visitors" and made no attempt to conceal their identities as professional military officers. Others passed themselves off as businessmen carrying ordinary, but fake, visas (Tanemura (ed.), 1979, p. 34). Regardless of the Japanese army's low opinion of the Singapore consulate's intelligence gathering prowess, it depended on the consulate's clandestine network of sympathizers to furnish daily support (lodging, food, transportation) to the army officers crisscrossing the Malaya Peninsula. All officers, legal or illegal, received backing from Japanese business, commercial, and industrial firms and relied on Foreign Ministry intelligence officers like Shinozaki Mamoru, attached to the Singapore consulate as a newspaperman in September 1939. The Japanese Foreign Ministry provided Shinozaki with a letter of appointment that attached him to the consulate, but Straits Settlement police would assert later that the consulate informed them that Shinozaki was an official member of its staff (Bridges, 1986, p. 24).

Lieutenant Colonel Tanikawa Kuzuo, head of the aviation section of the operations branch, arrived legally in Singapore during July 1940. He was to assess British air strength, the most dangerous threat to Japanese landing operations. Shinozaki, the self-described press secretary at the Japanese consulate, guided the colonel around Singapore, Mersing, and the southern parts of the Malay Peninsula. Tanikawa's reconnaissance convinced him that the RAF was overrated and also provided pivotal intelligence about the absence of defenses on the northwest side of Singapore Island. Takinawa later reconnoitered the west coast accompanied by two other Japanese army officers; apparently military attachés assigned to the Singapore consulate. (Yamamoto, 2016, pp. 204–205).

Tanikawa and his companions also met with Japanese residents along the way, stayed at Japanese-owned inns, ate at Japanese-owned restaurants, enjoyed logistic support from Japanese-owned companies, and used the Singapore consulate to send their intelligence to Tokyo. The Japanese consul on Penang arranged for the three officers to stay at the Japanese-owned Kobe Hotel, a suspected "safe-house" for Japanese agents in Kuala Lumpur. Special Branch detectives observed the trio meet with Watanabe Toru, who was blacklisted as an "active spy" by the police[88] (TNA,

KV3/426, 45, 56). What they discussed was not known. Tanikawa next surveyed potential landing beaches in northern Malaya and southern Thailand, recommending Singora and Pattani in Thailand and Khota Baru on Malaya's east coast to Tokyo as the prime invasion beaches. His accurate and annotated sketch maps of Singapore's RAF bases and scaled diagrams of fortifications, bunkers, and pillboxes went to Tokyo in the Singapore consulate's diplomatic pouch carrying the disclaimer: "These diagrams via the Singapore consulate are materials from our [AGS] investigations"[89] (JCAR Ref. No. C14110611000).

Tanikawa's initial skepticism about striking south evaporated during his travels and he returned to Tokyo on August 9 convinced that the operation could succeed (Gunjishi gakkai (eds.), 1998, p. 17, entry for August 9, 1940). Other doubters like Major Okamura Masayuki, who spent two months reconnoitering the Netherlands East Indies, similarly saw their concerns vanish and became fervent converts to the new strategy[90] (Hata et al. (eds.), 1963, p. 177). On August 15, six days after Tanikawa's return, the AGS operations branch, based on his reports, submitted its first comprehensive draft plan for southern operations against British, Dutch, and, if necessary, American colonies in Asia (Yamamoto, 2016, pp. 224–225).

During Tanikawa's intelligence gathering expedition, in Japan anti-British spy mania reached a crescendo, with reverberations felt in Singapore. In mid-July Japanese special higher police (tokkō-tai) arrested fourteen British subjects living in Japan as spies. During interrogation, the British reporter for the Reuters News Agency somehow fell from a second story window to his death. The irate British ambassador to Japan demanded reprisals, and on August 1 the prime minister approved the arrest of Japanese subjects then in British territory. In order to prevent indiscriminate retaliation from spiraling out of control, the cabinet insisted there be actual grounds for arrest and that targeted Japanese be relatively unimportant[91] (TNA, CAB 65/8/29).

Three days later Singapore Special Branch police detained Kobayashi Ishirō, *Dōmei* correspondent and lately manager of the Eastern News Agency, in a tit-for-tat move (Bridges, 1986, pp. 19–20). The special police already had Kobayashi under surveillance, but London had previously forbidden any move against him because of the international situation. Now authorized by the government, they arrested Kobayashi under Defense Regulations, alleging that he had circulated false stories about unrest among Indian troops garrisoning Singapore and that his outspoken anti-colonial opinions constituted a subversive verbal propaganda campaign. Special Branch detectives searched Kobayashi's home and newspaper offices, but contrary to expectations found nothing incriminating. Authorities released him from jail on September 21, contingent upon an undisclosed arrangement that he would leave the colony. Kobayashi complied, telling reporters that he was back to work and that he was well treated during his detention[92] (TNA, KV3/426, 121; "Japanese Detained," The *Malaya Tribune*, August 5, 1940, p. 3). Neither his arrest nor release got much newspaper play, being overshadowed by the detention of several Japanese in London and in Burma. During the Kobayashi affair, however, Special Branch uncovered a serious case of Japanese espionage in Singapore that foreshadowed Japan's increasingly bold spying efforts throughout Malaya.

4
Another Singapore spy scandal

On August 1, 1940, the AGS established the Southern Section (Nanpō han) within the European/Americas Branch, Intelligence Division. Like their operations branch counterparts, Japanese military intelligence officers had little knowledge, secret or otherwise, about Malaya because they traditionally targeted the Soviet Union and the Philippines. Now they found themselves sent to Malaya, the Netherlands East Indies, and Thailand as a military intelligence network spread throughout the West's colonial empires in Southeast Asia[93] (Sugita, 1987, p. 145).

On September 10, Shinozaki met two Japanese staff officers who had recently arrived in Singapore and guided them around the island. Special Branch detectives trailing the pair definitively identified them as two "middle rank Japanese officers" (Bridges, 1986, p. 25). Shinozaki's postwar memoir identified the pair as Tanikawa and Captain Kunitake Teruhito, but Tanikawa had returned to Tokyo the previous day. Kunitake was supposed to accompany Tanikawa to Singapore, but the British embassy in Tokyo pigeonholed his visa application, thereby delaying his departure (Kunitake, 1988, p. 463). The two traveling officers were likely newly promoted Major Satō Tokutarō, an aviation expert, and Lieutenant Colonel Yahara, then attached to Imperial General

Headquarters, both of whom entered Malaya in September 1940 (BBKS, 1985, p. 27).

Since his arrival at the consulate, Shinozaki had tried to organize a clandestine network to collect intelligence about the Singapore naval base. He sought to recruit British enlisted servicemen stationed at the base as spies. According to the police, he worked diligently over time, mostly by himself, to contact enlisted ranks of the three Services in order to harvest military intelligence[94] (TNA, KV3/426, 122). Shinozaki's unimaginative methods to recruit spies exposed him to the police. He approached passing uniformed servicemen near bustling *Chūō dōri* and invited them to dances or parties, popular events anytime in Singapore but even more-so now that the British Empire was at war with Germany.

Shinozaki steered those who agreed to the nearby Sakura Hotel where he and his mistress, Yamakawa Atsuko, threw large, raucous parties designed to attract servicemen. Free beer, free cigarettes, and free snacks put the crowd at ease. Soldiers, sailors, and airmen mixed on familiar terms with Shinozaki, and several uniformed servicemen were apparently regulars at the get-togethers. The only anomaly one noticed was the large number of Japanese men and women in the room. People came and went, and anyone was free to leave. Shinozaki walked departing service newcomers to the street and encouraged them to come again, or better still visit him for a beer at the Sakura's bar when off-duty. He often handed out Malay five-dollar bills, substantially more than the serviceman's daily wage, and reminded the soldiers to stay in touch. Very few servicemen took up his offer to visit him at the Sakura Hotel.

One who did was Gunner Frank Gardner, 31st Heavy Battery, who met Shinozaki while walking past the fashionable Adelphi Hotel in late December 1939. A car stopped behind him and out stepped Shinozaki with two attractive Japanese women. He asked if Gardner would like to attend a dance at the Adelphi, a place Gardner could otherwise neither afford nor be admitted to, and the three entered the hotel as Shinozaki's guests. Parties were always popular occasions, and social organizations and society matrons did their part for the war effort by opening their doors to the enlisted servicemen. The Y.W.C.A., for example, sponsored the Adelphi Hotel dance. News of parties at private homes in chic neighborhoods, serving free beer and spirits, reached servicemen by word-of-mouth. Shinozaki was often a guest or welcome drop-in at many such parties, and used the opportunity to search for possible recruits.

When Gardner left the Adelphi, Shinozaki accompanied him outside, gave Gardner his card, and invited the gunner to visit him at the Sakura Hotel. Gardner was ripe for recruitment. A lonely man with few, if any, friends in his unit, Gardner despised the army and was always short of money. A few days later, the two met in a private room at the Sakura where more free beer and cigarettes awaited. As they drank, smoked, and chatted, Shinozaki questioned Gardner about the state of the British forces in Singapore. Gardner openly provided whatever limited information he could[95] (ST, October 24, 1940, p. 11 and ST, November 19, 1940, p. 11). The special police would later acknowledge that he gave Shinozaki little military information of any value[96] (TNA, KV3/426, 122).

Nevertheless, Shinozaki continued to meet with Gardner, pay him, and assign him routine errands. Perhaps Gardner's greatest value was his ability to courier small packages to places where Japanese were routinely searched but where uniformed servicemen moved freely, like the Harbour Board; or where Japanese would be too conspicuous, say loitering around the lobby of the Union Building. Shinozaki and Gardner continued to meet at the Sakura Hotel until Gardner's hospitalization for a throat infection ended the sessions. Shinozaki moved out of the hotel in March 1940 and the parties stopped. Although Shinozaki shifted all his meetings to the nearby Japanese consulate, where he and Gardner reunited during the summer of 1940, he still used the Sakura as a convenient cut-out location to screen potential visitors ("Japanese Charged," ST, October 24, 1940, p. 11).

Around mid-July, based on confidential information, Special Branch's Japanese Section head Alan Blades ordered a special branch detective to tail Gardner. ("Shinozaki Described as a 'Press Clerk,'" ST, November 20, 1940, p. 12). Singapore's Special Branch simultaneously launched a "careful and methodical" investigation, hoping to ensnare an espionage ring that implicated senior officials of the Singapore consulate[97] (TNA, KV3/426, 122). The disappointing result, however, produced sufficient evidence to implicate a single soldier: Gunner Gardner. The special police later argued that had the government granted them full powers they would have caught a least one other important "Japanese consulate spy"[98] (TNA, KV3/426, 122).

A Malay detective assigned to follow Shinozaki saw him exchanging notes with a British serviceman outside the hotel and trailed the soldier back to his base. Security officials then arranged for a unit muster the following day. As the troops passed in review, the detective identified Royal Artillery Gunner Gardner. A few days later, on August 2, an undercover detective detained Gardner near the Sakura Hotel and delivered him to Special Branch where he was held incommunicado. The ostensible reason was to avoid alerting Shinozaki, who was still free, to the exposure of his spy-ring, but the special police also hoped to entrap the counsel-general's private secretary, Nagayama Shunzō, who they believed was resident spymaster at the consulate[99] (ST, October 24, 1940, p. 11 and ST, November 23, 1940, p. 11).

Gardner freely admitted to Blades that he had been passing information to Shinozaki since December 1939. Armed with this new information, Singapore requested the Colonial Office's permission to take action against Shinozaki. While Singapore officials awaited a response, Gardner candidly answered questions during his three-week detainment, but he knew so little that the police were unable to produce sufficient evidence for further indictments of enlisted servicemen[100] (Bridges, 1986, pp. 25–26; TNA, KV3/426, 122). Unable to detain Gardner indefinitely, the police formally arrested him on August 25. After receiving the Colonial Office's permission, on September 21 Special Branch detectives arrested Shinozaki and Yamakawa Atsuko as Gardner's accomplices. Before the preliminary hearing into Shinozaki's charges, however, Yamakawa's offense was discharged because of insufficient evidence. This was simply a legal convenience; authorities had not dropped the charges against her and could still recall her to stand trial[101] (Bridges, 1986, p. 25; ST, 21 Nov 1940, p. 11 & ST, 23 Nov 1940, p. 11). In similar fashion, police officially dated Gardner's arrest retroactive to August 25, meaning administratively that Special Branch had never held him in custody.

After his arrest and from the police station, Shinozaki contacted Toyoda Kaoru, the Japanese consul-general in Singapore, who immediately came to the station. He then escorted Shinozaki along with Special Branch detectives back to the consulate, an imposing red-roofed, two-story white Victorian villa overlooking *Chūō dōri*. Upon entering the villa's large circular foyer, Shinozaki bolted to a nearby room, picked up a sealed envelope, and tossed it to Nagayama Shunzō, the consul general's private secretary. Three Special Branch detectives wrestled the envelope from Nagayama, seized several of Shinozaki's files, and stopped another consular official from flushing a partially burned letter down the toilet.[102]

The confiscated documents implicated Nagayama in espionage, but senior British authorities, for diplomatic and intelligence reasons, opted not to pursue his case and instructed the Special Police to withhold any action against him pending further instructions. They exercised similar restraint by turning a blind eye when Toyoda later smuggled Nagayama out of Singapore to the Netherlands East Indies, from whence he returned to Japan[103] (TNA, KV3/426, 121, 124). Likewise, the Japanese Foreign Ministry in Tokyo backed off its initial threats to retaliate against vulnerable British consulate staff in the face of unwavering British determination to try Shinozaki in open court. Tokyo instead wrote off Shinozaki, ultimately notifying British Ambassador Craigie that if Shinozaki did anything, he did so as an individual and not as a member of the foreign service (Bridges, 1986, pp. 26–27).

Singapore authorities lacked evidence that implicated either Major Satō or Lieutenant Colonel Yahara in the consulate's spy ring and could not arrest them. The Japanese consulate similarly avoided retribution because London was unwilling to restrict its activities, fearing Japanese retaliation against British diplomatic legations in Japanese-controlled territories (Best, 2002, p. 181). Colonial authorities instead resorted to a highly publicized four-day trial and a harsh punishment to make an example of Shinozaki.

That November an assize court convicted Shinozaki of espionage for collecting military information and reports of troop movements "that might be useful to a foreign power." He was sentenced to three years imprisonment and fined 1,000 Malay dollars[104] ("Shinozaki Convicted," ST, November 23, 1940, p. 11; TNA, KV3/426, 122). Fallout also tainted Kashiwabara Kitsuji, a reporter for a local Japanese newspaper and one of Shinozaki's sources. Kashiwabara was arrested under the Official Secrets Act for allegedly passing information to Shinozaki, and though he denied the charges he was sentenced to three months hard labor followed by deportation[105] (Bridges, 1986, p. 26; TNA, KV3/ 426, 124). The brawl at the consulate discredited Toyoda,[106] who departed Singapore on November 2 and was replaced by the even more aggressive Consul General Tsurumi Ken, described by an American journalist "as a man with the air of a good fellow and the eyes of a cut-throat" (Allen, 1991, p. 88). Early in 1941 a court-martial sentenced Gardner to a lengthy prison term and discharge with ignominy. He had passed little more than barracks gossip, although he also had admitted having once smuggled a packet for Shinozaki past an inspection checkpoint at Empire

Dock[107] (TNA, KV3/426, 117; "Japanese Charged," ST, October 24, 1940, p. 11).

Unlike with the Kaseda affair, London and Singapore authorities encouraged detailed and extensive press reporting of Gardner's trial, including extended testimony. The contrast between the hard-nosed British action in 1940 and the low-key approach in 1934 brought into sharp relief the deterioration of Anglo-Japanese relations. Earlier self-imposed restraint designed not to embarrass Japan gave way to a deliberate policy designed to humiliate Tokyo, publicize Japanese spying, and, by meting out severe punishments, exert "a salutary effect on the Japanese Consul-General" and Japanese spies in the colony[108] (TNA, KV3/426, 117).

The Shinozaki incident did appear to temporarily inhibit Japanese spying in Singapore. The security police reported a single espionage incident during November 1940: the entrapment of a Chinese technician employed at the Singapore base who was trying to sell a blueprint of a British submarine propeller to anyone who might be interested. In January 1941, detectives arrested a Japanese seaman aboard a Japanese merchant ship for making sketches in a prohibited zone while entering Singapore harbor. He was sentenced to nine months hard labor and deportation (TNA, KV3/426, 117). Singapore seemed more secure, but only because the Japanese had shifted their major espionage effort to neighboring Thailand.

5

The Imperial Japanese Army takes charge

British agent and informer reports from Thailand grew more alarming, underscoring as they did the Japanese danger in that nation. The Japanese military, working closely with Tamura at the Bangkok consulate, infiltrated scores of undercover agents carrying fake documents. In early September 1940, about ten Japanese—supposedly businessmen or tourists with seemingly authentic visas, but actually undercover army general staff officers—arrived in Bangkok and then proceeded to roam around the Thai countryside brashly gathering intelligence about airfields, terrain, and beach conditions (Yoshimura, 1981, p. 216; Reynolds, 1994, pp. 65–66). Around the same time, Lieutenant Commander Inami Takao, deputy commander of a naval special base force unit at Amoy in south China, entered Thailand on false papers to organize and train a small plainclothes military detachment (Tomono, 1983, p. 140). Hard-pressed in the European war, the British Chiefs of Staff acknowledged in early November that their available forces could neither prevent a Japanese military move into Thailand nor exert effective military pressure on the

Thai government to resist such an invasion[109] (TNA, CAB 80/22/ 6). Tokyo was soon made aware of this glaring British weakness.

On the morning of November 11, 1940, the German commerce raider Atlantis intercepted the British merchantman *Automedon* in the Indian Ocean. A German boarding party searched the ship and confiscated top-secret documents, including the British chiefs' August 12, 1940, appreciation of the situation in the East Asia. The British chief's appraisal recommended avoiding an open clash with Japan, even if Japanese forces invaded French Indochina and Thailand, because matching the German and Italian navies in European waters made it "temporarily impossible" for the Admiralty to dispatch a fleet to East Asia (Farrell, 2015, p. 266; War History Branch, 1963, pp. 540, 542, 544).

Anxious to get Japan into the war against Britain, Berlin passed this intelligence windfall to Tokyo, where the revelations quickly influenced Japanese policy decisions. The December 27, 1940, Liaison Conference, held between representatives of Imperial General Headquarters and the civilian cabinet, discussed a possible move into French Indochina. Navy Minister Oikawa Koshirō referred to "secretly obtained documents" that revealed Britain would not go to war if Japan stopped after occupying Indochina, but a Japanese push into the Netherlands East Indies would mean war. Reports from Japanese spies in London reinforced Tokyo's awareness of British passivity regarding Thailand and of its overall military weakness in the region, encouraging a more aggressive Japanese espionage campaign throughout Southeast Asia[110] (Sanbō honbu henshū, 1967, p. 157; Farrell, 2015, pp. 266–268; Yamamoto, 2016, pp. 230–231).

As Tokyo edged closer to war and more and more Japanese army officers converged on Bangkok, Thailand emerged as the forward operating base for regional espionage. In January 1941, the AGS, Intelligence Department, deployed Major Aoyama Waichi to Bangkok on a one-month assignment. Two army communications specialists accompanied him. The trio set up a signals intercept site and, aided by Tamura, intercepted British diplomatic and military cables transmitted from Singapore (BBKS, 1984, 143). Allied cryptanalysts monitored Aoyama' return to Bangkok in mid-June to intercept RAF air-ground communications and related RAF radio traffic on a permanent basis (DoD, 1978, vol. 5, p. 6).

During January 1941, Thai and French forces had clashed over a disputed boundary. Tokyo expected that in exchange for supporting Bangkok's claims, Thai authorities would allow the Japanese army free passage through Thailand. Colonel Manaki Takanobu headed the Japanese delegation to the Thai-French Indochina border commission meetings held April to June 1941, then detached a team of officers and NCOs from his official diplomatic retinue to scout landing beaches at Singora in Thailand and Khota Baru in British Malaya (Rikusenshi kenkyū fukyūkai (eds.), 1966, p. 10; Reynolds, 1994, pp. 44–45).

All intelligence flowed to Taiwan, which became the center for Japanese operational planning for a Malaya campaign. On Christmas Day 1940, the AGS had activated Taiwan Army Unit 82, the so-called Taiwan Army Research Bureau, to gather and assess intelligence in order to develop a tropical warfare doctrine. Colonel Hayashi Yoshihide was the nominal head, but his deputy, Lieutenant Colonel Tsuji Masanobu, was in charge

(Tsuji, 1993, pp. 5–7; Yamamoto, 2016, pp. 273–274, 244–245). Tsuji was a fire-eater, ready to rush headlong into any situation. He could get things done because, unlike most Japanese, he acted independently without benefit of a group consensus. To some officers Tsuji was the "God of Operations"; to others he was rash, rude, and ruthless with soldiers' lives.

Under a Japanese governor general, Taiwan was the keystone of Japan's southern region expertise that enabled Tsuji to assemble a wealth of local civilian talent and draw on resources from government, commercial, academic, and financial institutions. ISK had a major branch office in Taipei and tapped its subsidiaries throughout Southeast Asia for additional know-how. The Bank of Taiwan was the only Japanese bank with branches throughout Southeast Asia, allowing it to transfer (or launder) operational funds to agents. The South Seas Association's Taiwan office was the most important of its overseas locations, active not only on Taiwan but also throughout the region (Peattie, 1996, p. 189). Trading companies like Mitsui and Mitsubishi were well represented, and there was also the ubiquitous *Dōmei* correspondent. The army recalled several reserve officers whose civilian careers included working for Japanese-owned trading companies in Singapore as well as Japanese mining, plantation, and transportation concerns in northern Malaya. Back on active duty, the reservists provided the AGS with a small but highly knowledgeable cadre of Malaya specialists. For example, First Lieutenant Fujiwara Shizuo, a long-time civilian resident of Malaya with a Japanese trading company, was a recalled reserve intelligence officer assigned to the AGS and then ordered to Thailand (Sugita, 1987, p. 216).

Unit 82 only had about 30 members: clerks, NCOs, and officers, including several officers who posed as civilian technicians to attend conferences or specialized lectures about Malaya. Genuine civilian participants knew enough to steer clear of the technicians, who looked out of place with their closely cropped military haircuts and ill-fitting civilian suits. No one dared question the ultimate purpose of the research (Tsuji, 1993, p. 2; Asaeda, 1983, pp. 117–118).

Unit 82 was one cog in the Japanese army's hastily augmented covert intelligence probe spreading throughout Southeast Asia. The Japanese army demanded specific tactical and operational intelligence about Malaya that only trained observers and experienced professional agents could supply. It dispatched confident and capable military professionals under orders to collect on-the-spot intelligence about specific targets that would be used in campaign planning and execution. These professionals analyzed landing beaches in southern Thailand and conducted terrain studies of routes from the beachheads that opened the way to northern and western Malaya; sites of the key opening battles. In other words, these military officers were rehearsing their tactics on the ground where their soldiers would soon fight.

Japanese expatriates in Malaya intentionally or unintentionally facilitated their missions. Army officers followed the pattern laid down by their predecessors, again relying on the Japanese-owned companies for transportation, guides, interpreters, and commercial intelligence. They depended less on the consulate's staff to guide them around Singapore and more on the consulate's powerful transmitter to radio their intelligence quickly to army headquarters in Tokyo. In the rugged rural areas on the Malaya Peninsula, they again sought and received sustenance from the Ōuchi-constructed local centers that provided their daily needs for food and lodging secure from outsiders.

The experience had by Captain Kunitake Teruhito, operations branch staff officer, was typical of this second wave of agents. In January 1941, Kunitake finally departed Tokyo for his long-delayed trip to Southeast Asia. He entered Malaya with a proper visa, although other accounts claim that he crossed the border as an "illegal" under diplomatic cover, or in Special Branch police jargon a "diplomatic visitor"[111] (Kunitake, 1988, p. 463). From January through March 1941, Kunitake conducted an extensive and thorough terrain reconnaissance in French Indochina, Thailand, and Malaya with an eye on potential airfield sites, landing beaches, and road and rail conditions. He entered Malaya from Thailand and was likely accompanied by Shimanuki Takeo, a consular official since May 1938 whose duties included codes and cables. Together they boarded a Singapore bound train at the border, getting off here and there along the way to make more detailed observations.

Counsel-General Tsurumi then showed Kunitake around Singapore and its northern approaches and accompanied Kunitake on his reconnaissance of the east coast towns of Endau and Mersing, presumably under Special Branch surveillance the entire time. Kunitake next retraced the route northward, this time by automobile, which allowed him to stop wherever he wanted along the west coast trunk road. At Panang, *Dainan konsu*, an established Japanese transportation and construction company headquartered in Saigon with branches throughout

Indochina and Thailand, provided him with a pilot and a small plane to fly over northwest Malaya, landing and taking off from several civilian or shared-use military airdromes. He visited local Japanese along his route, stayed at Japanese-owned inns, enjoyed logistic support from Japanese trading companies, and, like his predecessors, avoided carrying any scrap of paper that the British might use as a pretext to arrest him. Local undercover agents likely couriered his notes and sketches to the Singapore consulate, which in turn forwarded them to Tokyo for distribution to Unit 82 (Kunitake, 1988, pp. 463–466).

Kunitake returned to Japan convinced that large units could operate in Malaya and melded his and Tanikawa's findings into an April 1941 "Intelligence Report of British Malaya" filled with detailed maps complemented by specifics about the number and strength of British garrisons, gun batteries, and fortifications. The report undergirded operational planning for the Malaya campaign, and Unit 82 rapidly incorporated it into its voluminous preliminary report issued in late April. Unit 82's next and final late June report went to 25th Army Headquarters, activated that same month for Malaya operations. Shortly afterwards in August, Unit 82 shut down as the army shifted from planning to active preparation for war (Yamamoto, 2016, pp. 274–276, 278; Tsuji, 1993, p. 6). As for Kunitake, he was reassigned as the Malaya specialist to the Southern Region section, where his team devised equipment modifications, training routines, shipping schedules, and logistical tables for the Malaya operation. His success and ability brought him to the attention of General Yamashita Tomoyuki, who later had Kunitake reassigned to his 25th Army staff (Kunitake, 1988, pp. 463–466).

The British were well aware of Kunitake's spying because FECB cryptanalysts had deciphered, among other cables, Shimanuki's mid-February 1941 report to Tokyo on the thoroughness of Kunitake's reconnaissance of Malaya's northern defenses (Elphick and Smith, 1994, p. 138). This deciphering was possible because the previous September a handful of American cryptanalysts had solved the Japanese diplomatic encryption, in effect by reverse engineering the system through a specially constructed analogue device, the now-famous Purple Machine. In late January or early February 1941, the United States provided three copies of the Purple Machine to Britain as part of a communications intelligence sharing agreement (Hanyok, 2008, p. 10). Shortly thereafter, London sent FECB a Purple Machine (NSA, Benson, 1997, p. 20; Best, 2002, pp. 173–174). Once again Singapore's highest authorities were privy to Japan's highest diplomatic secrets. As was the consistent governing policy, rather than expose this vital intelligence source, British authorities took no action against Kunitake or Shimanuki.

These latest Japanese intelligence probes did, however, garner British respect. By mid-1941, the FECB commented on the improved quality and accuracy of intelligence reporting by the Japanese Consul General in Singapore. The intelligence sent by the consulate to Tokyo was correct regarding "the arrival of reinforcements, munitions and armaments, movements and composition of Military and R.A.F. units and movements of H. M. Ships in local waters." Counterintelligence police credited insider leaks from spies for the improvement, although FECB contended that inside sources were unnecessary because much of the "intelligence" was simply in front of one's nose[112] (TNA, KV3/426, 111).

Japanese observers on the north side of the Johore Straits, for example, allegedly kept Singapore's naval base under constant surveillance, but only in mid-June 1941 did the DSO announce that new defense area regulations would curtail such activities[113] (TNA, KV3/426, 113). In Penang, the Japanese government secretly funded a shop, managed by two SSA members, that overlooked new British defense works and troop barracks. Although both men were listed as "suspect and dangerous," not until November 1941 did Special Branch police order the two to leave the area[114] (TNA, KV3/426, 52 and 56). According to retrospective police analysis, this action and the clearing of the north bank of the Jahore Strait (separating Singapore Island from the Malay Peninsula) had come "too late to be of any real value." Put differently, potential spies in Malaya were not "removed soon enough or extensively enough from vital military areas"[115] (TNA, KV3/426, 99). To add to security headaches, the English-language press provided a running account of Australian and Indian reinforcements because official policy had initially encouraged editors to headline the arrival of major reinforcements in order to boost civilian morale.

Thousands of on-lookers along with military and Colonial Office dignitaries welcomed the highly publicized first increment of almost 6,000 Australian troops who arrived aboard the *Queen Mary* in mid-February 1941. As the year wore on and Anglo-Japanese relations worsened, official statements became less straightforward. On March 30, the Commander-in-Chief Far East, Air Marshal Sir Robert Brooke-Popham, announced the arrival of "crack fighter pilots" from the Battle of Britain, plus veteran British and Indian ground units. A month later, newspapers reported without further comment that large new forces and equipment had landed[116] (NYT, March 31, 1941, p. 5; NYT April 25, 41, p. 1). In mid-August the press briefly described, without further details, what it termed the largest reinforcement yet to reach Malaya[117](NYT, August 15, 1941, p. 10).

Tsurumi saw through the public relations strategy and notified Tokyo in October that:

> [I]n spite of the fact that troops are still arriving from Australia and India only very minor mention is made of it now. This would seem to indicate that although in February exaggerated reports were essential to give confidence to the people, now that defense measures have actually reached adequacy, there is no longer any need for doing so.[118]
>
> DoD, 1978, vol. 3-app, pp. A392–A393

Two weeks earlier Tsurumi had reported to Tokyo that the quality of RAF pilots was good, but their equipment and logistical support poor (Best, 2002, p. 184). The AGS Vice Chief of Staff's reply requested more intelligence about the RAF's organization in Malaya and details about its aerial formations, maneuvers, and tactics[119] (DoD, 1978, vol 4-app, p. A170). As it turned out, the Japanese army had a perfect spy in the perfect place to deliver such vital intelligence.

A renegade New Zealand officer embedded in the RAF's northern Malaya air bases provided his Japanese handlers with a running commentary on the colony's air defense system. Japanese intelligence had apparently recruited Captain Patrick Heenan in Tokyo during his "long leave" in the mid-1930s, probably with lures of cash and women. The 31-year-old Indian Army officer was a misfit; an embittered, hot-tempered bully; the kind of soldier routinely palmed off on other units in hopes that they would keep him. He continued to bounce around after his unit deployed to Malaya in early 1941, and that June found him at Alor Star as the 11th Division's air-liaison officer with the RAF[120] (Farrell, 2015, p. 332n19; Elphick and Smith, 1994). Heenan's pivotal position allowed him unhindered access to the RAF's order of battle in Malaya, as well as its codebooks, base defense plans, aerial tactics, and aerial counter-invasion measures. His routine duties took him to various RAF airfields in the northwest, and his mates were well aware of his womanizing in Georgetown and elsewhere. Heenan's carousing likely provided a convenient cover that allowed him to pass secrets to the resident Japanese consul in Penang or to contact Japanese agents, SSA members, and indigenous collaborators in the city. His Japanese controllers provided him with a radio transmitter, concealed in a communion set, that allowed him to send illicit radio messages to Japanese clandestine receiving sites in Thailand. Heenan also sold information on Khota Bharu's defense dispositions to Malay collaborators. Resentment may have fueled his treachery, but he never passed up the money[121] (TNA, KV3/426, 102, 67, 74; Elphick and Smith, 1994, pp. 120, 176, 195–197).

Japan's occupation of southern French Indochina in July 1941 provoked the United States into restricting exports and freezing Japanese assets. Tokyo promptly ordered all overseas commercial firms to reduce staff to a minimum. The end of Japanese commercial interests in Malaya created increasing uneasiness among Japanese residents and triggered a hasty exodus of those who could afford to leave. British police reports described scenes "culminating in a panic to get away" as those Japanese who had ticket money scrambled aboard every Japanese ship calling on ports in Malaya[122] (TNA, KV3/426, 113–114).

6

The Singapore consulate and fifth columns

Japanese residents may have been jamming ships to leave Malaya, but the Singapore consulate continued its espionage activities uninterrupted. By mid-June 1941, deciphered consular cable traffic revealed a "continuous stream of military and shipping intelligence through consuls" to Tokyo and was almost the only source the British had available to gauge "the extent and success of Japanese espionage"[123] (TNA, KV3/426, 116). Who was supplying intelligence about British reinforcements and troop movements, munitions and weapons, and unit organization to the consuls? Suspicion fell on the large Asian population that the British military employed, ranging from skilled technicians and mechanics in essential occupations to mess servants and gardeners in more ordinary jobs, along with a vast coolie labor force working for construction contractors[124] (TNA, KV3/426, 111).

In mid-October 1941, and again later that month, the head of Special Branch's Japanese Section and a representative from Far Eastern Security Section (FESS), FECB examined recent Japanese consular messages to ascertain their accuracy concerning the state of Malaya's defenses and, if possible, to identify potential sources who had access to such information. After checking their findings with the respective staff officers of the three Services, they concluded that a Japanese espionage ring depended on the Japanese consulate as a clearinghouse to collate raw data and to forward its finished military intelligence reports to the Army General Staff in Tokyo. According to the FECB director, "All Japanese residents in Malaya" were either directly or indirectly implicated in this organization, which covered all of Malaya, embraced "numerous individuals," and also used other Asians— Chinese, Malay, and Indian—as agents. The espionage network obtained the substance of its reports by observation, not the pilfering or compromise of official documents. The extent of the material suggested that different agents collected the information at different places and times, allowing analysts to give context to the finished product. Although the consulate had been passing intelligence for decades, its previous reports were usually inaccurate or too sporadic to demand counteraction. Now at a time of acute danger, it was producing accurate and valuable intelligence that placed British and Dominion forces at risk. Nevertheless, the combination of the fear of compromising vital Imperial and valuable local intelligence sources, absence of definitive evidence without exposing those special sources, complexity of the Japanese network, existing legislation, and limited counterespionage resources made it impossible to take effective action against the consulate[125] (TNA, KV3/426, 108).

Commander-in-Chief Far East Brooke-Popham, for instance, was unwilling as yet to recommend shutting down Japan's Singapore consulate (as had already been done in India) because that would eliminate the best intelligence source about Japanese espionage activities in Malaya then available to the British. It would also provoke Japanese retaliation, which was unpalatable to senior leaders in London who rightly regarded the Nazi German war machine as the mortal threat. The FECB director alternatively proposed confining all Japanese to their hometowns to prevent the information flow and implementing tough action against non-Japanese Asiatic agents using current defense regulations[126] (TNA, KV3/426, 109). London rejected such harsh measures, insisting the rule of law held precedence.

Although the FECB provided British military intelligence with unimpeachable intelligence about Japan's expanding espionage operations, the military services were unable to infiltrate the spy network. That June, Commander-in-Chief Far East notified the War Office that his command lacked information on the mechanics of Japanese espionage in Malaya and had few effective counter measures to combat subversion. Malaya Command, for example, had neither the equipment nor the technical organization to detect illicit radio transmitters broadcasting from Malaya or Singapore and was further handicapped by a lack of cooperation from civilian government departments[127] (TNA, KV3/426, 116 and 101). The pervasive friction between the military and Special Branch also retarded the counterintelligence effort on the eve of the war.

Service authorities had little confidence in and paid little attention to police reports compiled by officers who spent entire careers studying the Japanese espionage apparatus[128] (TNA, KV3/426, 72). As far as the police were concerned, the military Services' indifference to security affairs and their unwillingness to punish any security violation encouraged a lack of "security mindedness" that allowed loose-lipped officers to discuss classified information openly at their clubs, in shops, and with their wives, blissfully ignorant that eavesdroppers and spies among the large Asiatic population employed at British military bases throughout Malaya were listening. Both sides exchanged heated recriminations at the "stormy and controversial" November 11 security committee meeting[129] (TNA, KV3/426, 111, 105). Counterintelligence officers believed that they did the "dirty work" conducting underground investigations while the Services treated their hard-gained intelligence with "scant credence or attention," and instead sat back and did nothing. A contemporary observer remarked that such feelings were "eloquent of the general 'atmosphere' in Malaya before the Japanese showed their hand in December 1941"[130] (TNA, KV3/426, 105, 72).

The "continuous stream of military and shipping intelligence" detected by the British coincided with Japan's final preparations for war. Fresh and reliable data were incorporated into operational planning at a September 1941 planning conference. Japanese staff officers pored over detailed sketches and topographical maps to scale of Malaya and Singapore, annotated with precise details of the British order of battle and their tactical defensive positions along potential landing beaches and inland. Army officers believed 50,000 to 60,000 Indian and Australian troops had reinforced the English forces in Malaya since the outbreak of war in Europe in September 1939, making a total force of roughly 71,000, plus another 10,000 volunteers. They knew the size, location, organization, equipment, and mixed composition (Australian/British/Indian) of these forces. They also marked many of them as substandard.

According to the Japanese, during the pre-war era, Caucasian British units formed the backbone of Malaya's defense, but they had redeployed to Europe and been replaced by Indian and Australian units. The Australians frankly puzzled the Japanese army. Notorious for their lack of military discipline, they appeared to be an army of "the unemployed and scoundrels." Yet the Australians had fought courageously in the Near East and the 20,000 Australian troops in Malaya (actually around 15,000) could be expected to fight well. As for the Indians, many did not wish to fight Japan or harbored anti-British feelings. They were not serious opponents. The majority of the 11,000 British servicemen who remained in Malaya were fortress troops and, excepting one infantry brigade, inexperienced in field operations. The recently mobilized volunteer militia units, assigned to guard depots, preserve order, and conduct limited military activities, were disparaged out of hand. Besides numbers and unit effectiveness, the Japanese possessed technical details on enemy weapons and equipment[131] (JCAR Ref. No. C14110609900).

Japanese naval intelligence generally concurred with the army's estimates of Dominion land forces and contributed a strategic and operational assessment of the naval forces arrayed against Japan throughout the Southern Region. In mid-September 1941, the naval general staff's third department (Intelligence), eighth branch (Great Britain) regarded the naval threat as minimal. Singapore's vaunted naval base held only a few minor warships, and just two cruisers were in the region. These would be destroyed quickly as Japan gained control of the seas. Rapid reinforcements were possible, but the European war precluded the Royal Navy from dispatching a major fleet to Singapore.

Britain's improving prospects, however, vis-a-vis the Italian navy in the Mediterranean and strengthened counter-amphibious defenses against a German invasion, did enable London to deploy perhaps four warships to interfere with Japan's southward advance[132] (JCAR Ref. No. C14121193200). The Japanese would await the enemy fleet, engage it, and sink it in Indian or northern Australian waters (Yamamoto, 2016, p. 201).

Navy intelligence analysts also concluded that beginning in April 1941 the British had reinforced air and ground units on the Malay Peninsula and strongly fortified and strengthened Malaya's east coast and northern border, revealing their intention to defend the entire peninsula. Some of this recent intelligence about British border deployments likely came from Lieutenant Commander Inami, the undercover naval officer in Thailand, who again relied on fake travel documents to enter Malaya. He rode the train from the Thai border to Singapore accompanied by a young Japanese woman to complement his cover as a tourist. Inami and other undercover military agents reported in detail about British reinforcements along the Malaya-Thai border and the construction of pillboxes, barbed-wire obstacles, and minefields to defend possible landing beaches along the east coast (Tomono, 1983, p. 140). The navy also rigged a revolving movie camera inside the mast of one of Eifuku Tora's trawlers that in turn proceeded to film Singapore's fortifications from the seaward side (Asaeda, 1983, p. 117).

Army officers or "diplomatic visitors" had scouted potential landing beaches along the Malay and Thai coasts. They provided significant details about tidal conditions, coastline defenses, waterline fortifications and obstacles, and inland terrain leading off the beaches. Hand-drawn maps of the beach area that displayed recommended landing zones complemented their narratives[133] (JCAR Ref. No. C1400168600). Japanese troop commanders were confident that they could get their units ashore and defeat the enemy ground forces. Their greater concern was RAF warplanes bombing the vulnerable Japanese troop transports and cargo ships lying at anchor just offshore the invasion beaches.

Planners likewise regarded the RAF as the most serious threat to the imminent invasion. The Japanese were already familiar with permanent pre-war airfields like Alor Star, but the whereabouts and capabilities of the new fields under construction since 1937 remained a mystery. Considerable effort went into identifying the new airbases and aircraft reinforcements. By September 1941, Army officers possessed scaled and annotated maps with the locations of all RAF air bases in British Malaya; they also possessed renderings of those airdromes that included specific runway lengths and orientations as well as extensive ancillary information about fuel storage tanks, troop barracks, aircraft hangers, and any construction[134] (JCAR Ref. No. C14060168600). It is worth conjecturing about how the Japanese obtained such extensive intelligence.

It was impossible to construct advance airfield installations in complete secrecy. Indians, Japanese, or Malays living nearby could see that the British were clearing land for some purpose. Indians and Malays likely supplied some of the hardscrabble airfield laborers and later talked about work in their villages or towns. If townspeople saw uniformed soldiers directing work gangs, they could easily guess military construction of some sort was underway. Military personnel also apparently talked openly to local shopkeepers or workers about their assignments at the burgeoning base. Test flights by British military aircraft flying to and from the newly constructed landing runways confirmed their purpose. As the airstrips neared operational completion, Japanese businessmen assigned to district offices of large commercial companies like ISK, *Dainan konsu*, and so on, as well as South Seas Association members, might visit the location, stay at Japanese-owned establishments, and exchange small talk with long-time Japanese residents about recent changes in the area. Regional Japanese commercial companies, the quasi-official SSA, or possibly local Japan Association offices could also act as collection points to assemble this disparate, raw data and move it to the Singapore consulate to forward to Tokyo. If certain of these initial raw reports seemed promising, Tokyo might dispatch military specialists for firsthand, professional assessment of conditions in the suspect area. The officer–spies did not thrash blindly across the Malaya countryside. They knew exactly where they were going, why they were going, and what they were looking for. In this fashion, they determined which air bases could support bombers, which could support fighters, and which were of no value to them. They harvested intelligence, regardless of FECB's intent monitoring of Japanese military radio traffic and Special Branch's elevated security measures that restricted travel by Japanese and placed Japanese "tourists" under constant observation. The Singapore consulate faithfully cabled their polished findings to Tokyo, each another small tributary feeding the "continuous stream" of intelligence that FECB was deciphering.

Based on the recent comprehensive espionage campaign, Army intelligence estimated that in September 1941 the British had 150 combat aircraft, equally divided among bombers, fighters, and reconnaissance planes, and that they expected aerial reinforcements to double by December. It evaluated the Australian and British pilots as comparatively good but believed their flight training substandard[135] (JCAR Ref. No. C14110610300). The navy's eighth branch estimated that the British would have about 190 first-line combat aircraft directly committed to Malaya's defense by the end of 1941. Another 146 warplanes were available from fields in India, British Borneo, and the Andaman Islands[136] (JCAR Ref. No. C14121193200). Recall that the RAF actually had 158 combat aircraft available when the war broke out in Malaya.

Numerous agent reports described a well-developed and paved west coast road network running from the Thai border to Singapore. Its design (few sharp turns, few winding sections), exceptional width (as much as six meters), and first-class grading were ideal for heavy truck traffic carrying military equipment and supplies or for an infantry division on the march. Local spies or sympathizers cautioned that British demolition teams were setting demolition charges to destroy wooden bridges along the route, meaning that the Japanese would have to move fast to secure the bridges intact or assign additional field construction units to rebuild them. East coast roads were far inferior, being mostly gravel and flanked by rice paddies or swampland that confined units to a single narrow and flood-prone track. This accurately described the road and terrain conditions south of Khota Bharu. Such a route could at best support an infantry regiment and would require extra road repair crews and construction material during the rainy season (which began in November) even to accommodate that limited number of troops. Japanese and Malayan spies also supplied detailed information about which inland lateral roads could support large units. Staff planners applied military objectives to the road infrastructure to estimate time-and-distance projections. They determined that an unopposed advance of about 60 miles from the Thai border to Penang would take an infantry column five days, a motorized unit one day, and a flying column[137] three to four hours[138] (JCAR Ref. No. 14060168700). These figures provided a rough approximation of how quickly the army logisticians would have to push resupply forward along the roads and rails to keep pace with the advancing troops.

Japan's 1941 army, however, was not motorized, and depended more on horses and carts than trucks for the short haul of provisions. Railroads were the foundation for a logistics doctrine that held that multi-division operations could not be conducted outside a radius of 120 to 150 miles from a major resupply base. Singapore lay more than 500 miles from the projected landing beaches. Geography would force the Japanese to create supply depots along their route of advance and link the depots with the troops by rail. Preparation for such an undertaking required spies and agents to supply as much intelligence as possible about Malaya's rail network. Agents reported that major railroad lines were well developed along the commercial west coast while the few on the east coast lacked the infrastructure and capacity to support much more than a single division. Japanese military planners had accurate counts of rolling stock, locomotive engines, load capacities, and locations of coal supplies, water towers, and roundhouses[139] (JCAR Ref. No. C14060168800). Most of the "intelligence" came from open sources—almanacs, gazetteers, official and commercial annual reports, and so on—and the Japanese military attaché in Bangkok constantly forwarded updated eyewitness appreciations to Imperial General Headquarters. This wealth of detail enabled logistics staff officers to develop realistic timetables to ensure that resupply reached its intended forward units. Logisticians also appealed to operations officers (who traditionally scorned logistics and logisticians) to provide additional railway construction units to keep the rail lines open and the trains running regardless of weather, and to provide more infantry to prevent ground raids or air attacks on the vulnerable trains and rails[140] (JCAR Ref. No. C14060168800).

Somewhat surprisingly, there was scant information about jungle conditions, and that consisted mainly of encircling large swaths of Malaya with ovals indicating "jungle." These were useless on the small-scale maps of Malaya, as was the accompanying very brief narrative that encouraged troops to stay on coastal roads to avoid the deep jungle[141] (JCAR Ref. No. 14060168800). At a time when the army was training the invasion divisions for tropical warfare, the report's omission appears contradictory. It was understandable, however, because no one—ordinary citizens, spies, army officers, Japanese residents—went into the deep jungle, leaving it to the imagination of others to describe.

7

Final measures, the Singapore consulate, and the KAME

The September review found Tsuji assigned to the 25th Army under Headquarter which had deployed to Saigon during late July. Captain (soon to be Major) Asaeda Shigeharu arrived from Tokyo a few days after the assignment and reported to Tsuji, who ordered him to sneak into Malaya disguised as a coolie! Asaeda was stunned. Just a few days before, he had received verbal orders from Army Chief of Staff General Sugiyama Hajime to enter Thailand undercover to gather intelligence about the designated landings beaches. Asaeda (1983, pp. 117–121) quickly realized that he was the butt of Tsuji's perverse humor and soon after left for Thailand.[142]

Asaeda illegally entered Thailand masquerading as an agricultural technician working directly for the Governor General of Taiwan on an official study of rubber and teak groves. The AGS and foreign ministry arranged for a fake passport issued under an assumed name, and to complete the cover the foreign ministry used that alias when it posted his assignment in the Official Gazette. Asaeda drew funds from the Bank of Taiwan and administrative and logistical support from Japanese trading companies in

Thailand. Japanese employees of *Dainan konsu* (which had also helped Kunitake) always accompanied Asaeda during his work, including an interpreter fluent in Thai. He spent September and October inspecting rubber tree leaves near the Thai-Malaya border (but never entered Malaya), careful to maintain his cover because British counterintelligence teams were, more or less, openly tracking Japanese agents operating in southern Thailand, which to Asaeda seemed more like a British protectorate than a sovereign nation. He was not far wrong. British officers dressed as civilians carrying fake passports that identified them as businessmen were crossing into southern Thailand to conduct on-site reconnaissance and to keep a closer eye on their Japanese counterparts (Elphick and Smith, 1994, p. 144).

Asaeda's priority was to identify military airfields in Thailand that might allow Japanese army aircraft to cover the landing beaches that were beyond the range of Japanese-controlled airdromes in French Indochina. Few, if any, airstrips he saw could handle the constant and rigorous demands of operational aircraft, making it vital to seize intact the hard-surfaced RAF runways at Alor Star and Kota Bharu.

Asaeda's party also surveyed the rail and road network and the Thai beaches at Singora and Patani. ISK employees provided intelligence on east coast terrain conditions, and the company hosted an all-day outing on Singora's beaches that allowed Asaeda to make leisurely observations of beach and tide conditions (Asaeda, 1983, p. 122). He learned from local fishermen that high waves along Thailand's beaches during the northeast monsoon could play havoc with landing craft. On the other hand, he saw that defenses along the Thai coast seemed to consist of barbed wire entanglements and empty trenches. He also walked the track from Patani to the Malaya border, a route that outflanked British ground defenses and air bases north of Penang. Heavy vehicular traffic could not use the unpaved track running through jungle-clad mountains. But Asaeda realized that an infantry regiment could (Allen, 1991, p. 114). He returned to Tokyo in October to report his observations to the AGS. Three days later, he was on a plane back to 25th Army headquarters.

Shortly before the Japanese invasion, Asaeda boarded a 25th Army transport plane for a roundabout flight from French Indochina to Taiwan via Shanghai. At each stopover he distributed detailed topographical maps and intelligence updates to the divisional and regimental commanders leading the Malaya campaign.[143] Asaeda then accompanied the 42d Infantry Regiment aboard ship, landed with it at Patani on December 8, and lent the regiment his expertise as it advanced along the track toward the Malay border that he previously reconnoitered. The next afternoon, the vanguard linked up with three undercover Japanese army officers, two ISK employees, and the "tiger of Malaya," a young expatriate Japanese bandit gang leader whose men served as guides and advance scouts[144] (Tomono, 1983, p. 137).

Asaeda was just one of many clandestine military operatives moved into the region during the latter half of 1941. In mid-August, the Foreign Ministry elevated the Bangkok consulate to embassy status, a move that improved its covert capability and explained the sudden influx of Japanese "businessmen" (Yoshimura, 1981, p. 217). A month earlier, Lieutenant Colonel Kadomatsu Shōichi, chief of the AGS 8th Section (covert operations), had visited Bangkok where Tamura had revealed his underground connections with Indian and Malay nationalists (Mercado, 2002, p. 26). In early September Kadomatsu ordered his subordinate Lieutenant Colonel Fujiwara Iwaichi to Thailand at the head of an eleven-man (including four civilians) undercover team to collect intelligence and subvert Indian troops stationed in northern Malaya (Fujiwara, 1983, p. 11; Rikusenshi kenkyū fukyūkai (eds.), 1966, p. 12). Everyone carried bogus passports and wore civilian clothes, but according to Fujiwara the tell-tale close-cropped military-style haircuts belied any disguise. The team's five junior officers and one non-commissioned officer were all graduates of the Nakano School, the army's training school for clandestine operations.

The army's Nakano School was an army intelligence facility opened in the spring of 1938 that trained active duty and reserve officers, as well as non-commissioned officers, in espionage tradecraft to fill a void by providing timely wartime field intelligence. In late 1941, it sent about ten graduates disguised as foreign ministry clerks, journalists, businessmen, and laborers to Thailand, Malaya, and the Netherlands East Indies, usually for short-term assignments, where they worked with the military attachés assigned to the consulates (Kuwada, 1996, p. 225; Peattie, 1996, pp. 226–227; Reynolds, 1994, p. 66). Two clerks posted to the newly opened Japanese consulate at Singora near the Thai-Malaya border were army officers and Nakano school graduates who gathered intelligence on beach and tide conditions as well as roads and bridges near the designated landing sites. Another officer posed as a foreign ministry official, and yet another as a *Dainan konsu* company employee (Fujiwara, 1983, pp. 20–21, 34; Kuwada, 1996, p. 226; Peattie, 1996, pp. 225–

227). The three undercover army officers that Asaeda and the 42d Infantry met along met the Patani track were members of Fujiwara's network.

Japanese army reconnaissance aircraft also openly violated the colony's air space. Tsuji commandeered a pilot from a recently arrived reconnaissance squadron and made two unauthorized flights over Khota Baru and northern Malaya. Army medium bombers staging from Saigon began systematic overflights in early November. Three twin-engine unmarked aircraft (ground crews had painted over the trademark red disc markings) flying at 20,000 feet photographed Khota Baru and other key locations in northern Malaya. It is uncertain whether the British were aware of these violations, but Japanese pilots reported no reaction from the ground (Tsuji, 1993, pp. 35–36; Zadankai, 1983, pp. 355–356).

This military activity targeted northern Malaya, while in Singapore Consul General Tsurumi, acting on a May directive from the foreign ministry, cultivated anti-British or anti-colonial Malays to extend Japan's spy network throughout the colony and create a much larger, and potentially more seditious, Malay fifth column. The alliance with disaffected Malays enabled the Japanese to conduct an espionage and subversion campaign far disproportionate to their tiny numbers. Only a tiny minority of Japanese military officers and civilian officials believed the government's rhetoric about "liberating" Asian colonies from Western imperialist domination. Most regarded the West's colonies in Asia, and their Asian populations, as subjects of the expanding Japanese empire. In the short term, the "liberated territories" would supply the essential raw materials to fuel Tokyo's war engine and in the longer term they would be incorporated into an Asian co-prosperity sphere under Japanese leadership. One brand of colonialism replaced another. The hypocrisy was not lost on Asian nationalists who accepted Japanese prewar assistance and subsequently collaborated with their latest conquerors to keep alive opportunities for their national goal of independence.

Tsurumi recruited several Japanese residents of Singapore to guide the clandestine operation. Among the other Japanese involved were T. John Fujii, Ishikawa Keishu, Kaite Yoshi, Nagano Shohei, and Watanabe Itaru. Fujii had been born in Japan but educated in the United States. In September 1938 he joined the New York bureau of the *Asahi Shimbun* and in February 1939 he was recruited by a Japanese consular official in New York to join the staff of the Singapore *Herald*. The Colonial Office in London reported that he had been sent to Singapore for "subversive work"[145] (Goodman, 2000, p. 415; TNA, KV/426, 43).

Ishikawa owned a small trading company and channeled consulate funds to the vernacular Malay newspaper in the form of paid advertisements, usually with pro-Japanese themes. Kaite was the resident *Dōmei* correspondent and paymaster for the consulate's subversive campaign. Nagano owned the daily Japanese newspaper, Singapore *Nippo*, and was the front man for the English language Singapore *Herald*, which was financed by the Japanese government. He had been a contact of Dr Ōuchi and received an annual 24,000 yen ($12,000 U.S.) subvention from the Japanese consul general. Watanabe was a medical doctor at a Singapore Dohjin Hospital, a Japanese private hospital built exclusively for Japanese residents and regarded by police as a propaganda arm of the Japanese government[146] (TNA, KV3/426, 46, 51, 56).

Kaite introduced Tsurumi to Ibrahim bin Taji Ya'ocob, the founder and leader of the Kesatuan Melayu Muda (KMM) (Malaya Youth League), which was an officially registered nation-wide association of about 1,000 young Malay men.[147] The 30-year-old Malayan had founded the KMM in 1937 after being forced from his reporting job because of his outspoken criticism of British colonial rule. Ostensibly a social organization, the KMM was organized on a provincial basis with cells throughout Malaya, but centrally controlled by Ibrahim from Singapore. The association operated the *Warta Malaya*, the most important vernacular Malay newspaper in Singapore, and Ibrahim served as managing editor. Ibrahim's job and his KMM position were excellent covers that enabled him to move freely around Malaya to recruit members for his KMM, collect military information for the Japanese, and secure clients for his newspaper[148] (TNA, KV3/426, 78 and 106).

Ibrahim was anti-colonialist and anti-British, but above all he was a zealous Malay nationalist. He played the British, working as a Special Branch agent "for some considerable time," and manipulated Tsurumi into financing his acquisition of *Warta Malaya*. Kaite served as the conduit for the transaction that passed the consulate's money to Ibrahim for the purchase. The consulate also provided a plush subsidy that underwrote the newspaper's operating budget and funded routine KMM expenses through advertisements placed in *Warta Malaya*. Ishikawa's trading company laundered consulate money into generous advertising dollars (considered bribes by the British) for the newspaper that in exchange printed Dr. Watanabe's pro-

Japanese and thinly veiled anti-British propaganda, usually along the lines that Japanese help was necessary to achieve Malayans' independence goals[149] (TNA, KV3/426, 79). These were sound investments. A vernacular newspaper had obvious propaganda advantages and the Japanese likely expected *Warta Malaya* would provide favorable coverage during a future occupation of Malaya.

Sometime in July or August, Tsurumi and Ibrahim organized a secret, internal KMM cell that the Japanese called KAME (tortoise) to provide intelligence and assistance to the Japanese military during an invasion. KAME members would then help to administer and pacify places under Japanese occupation[150] (TNA, KV3/426, 89). KAME relied on the KMM's legal cells to extend its influence throughout Malaya. British authorities accurately described it as a "parasitic organization" that existed illegally by organizing itself around a small nucleus of radical Malays within the legitimately registered KMM who were willing to work with the Japanese. Most KMM members, who included middle-class schoolmasters, minor officials, and enlisted serviceman, were unaware of KAME and Ibrahim's aims; indeed, some later harshly condemned his machinations. Still, Ibrahim connected Japan and the KMM while Kaite was Ibrahim's contact with the consular mission, completing the link between the Japanese and a "rather loose but nevertheless widespread 'Fifth Column' in Malaya"[151] (TNA, KV3/426, 78–79, 106, 47).

FECB knew from messages it had deciphered during April and May that Tokyo had directed Consul-General Tsurumi to intensify subversive efforts. FECB later read his periodic updates to Tokyo on KAME's progress; these updates unmasked the Japanese role in Ibrahim's conspiracy to recruit young Malays for espionage, distribution of anti-British propaganda, and assistance to the Japanese military (Best, 2002, p. 184). Special Branch placed him under round-the-clock police surveillance.

KAME conspirators were spreading anti-colonial and pro-Japanese propaganda and preparing the groundwork for a general uprising of Malays in case of war. On September 11, 1941, Singapore Special Branch police arrested two Japanese SSA members, who were also KAME agents, for distributing seditious literature. They apparently implicated Kaite, who was already under surveillance as a KAME leader and paymaster for the group[152] (Peattie, 1996, p. 223; TNA, KV3/426, 47).

British authorities understood KAME as a Japanese-controlled fifth column, but a more apt characterization might be a Malay fifth column financed by Japan. Old Malaya hands discounted that possibility, attributing internal disloyalty to all Japanese residents *ipso facto* while believing "the Malays throughout the country were intensely loyal and perfectly satisfied with British rule... [being] naturally a lazy, kindly and not at all politically-minded people"[153] (TNA, KV3/426, 66). Sir Arthur Jelf, who in 1926 had organized the Special Branch police to deal with communist subversion, echoed the conventional colonial wisdom when he acknowledged that the Malays were not fond of the British, but insisted that "the easy-going Malay would hardly wish to disturb a system in which he was notoriously happy and prosperous"[154] (TNA, KV3/426, 71). Colonial officials failed to understand Ibrahim's nationalist appeal to young Malay activists, neither fully recognizing that the KMM's cells were an espionage and nascent sabotage network nor realizing that more extreme Malayan nationalists were willing to take a chance on the Japanese in order to rid themselves of British rule. Radical Malays, not the resident Japanese, were the more dangerous fifth-column.

In mid-November, intercepted Foreign Ministry cables divulged that Consul-General Tsurumi was to depart Singapore soon without an appointed successor in place. On his way out, Tsurumi updated Fujiwara's team in Bangkok on local conditions in Singapore and revealed the KAME fifth column. Tsurumi enthusiastically promoted KAME's use of Malay radicals to expand the Japanese intelligence network and further complicate British counterintelligence operations in southern Thailand. Fujiwara's operatives had already tapped disaffected Indians and Sikhs in Bangkok, previously cultivated by military attaché Tamura, to run espionage missions and foster subversion among Indian army units deployed in northern Malaya (Allen, 1991, p. 260). But he knew little about conditions in Singapore or southern Malaya. For whatever reasons, Tsurumi had waited until mid-November to update Fujiwara in Bangkok about the KMM's links to Japanese agents operating from the Singapore consulate, the KAME's national sedition campaign, and the still vague plans for a general uprising (Fujiwara, 1983, p. 41; Allen, 1991, p. 88). Shortly afterwards Fujiwara notified Ibrahim that war was imminent, perhaps as a desperate last-minute attempt to impose basic coordination of their mutual objective. Ibrahim promptly ordered KAME members to cooperate with Japanese troops and tried to alert Fujiwara to his latest plans (Fujiwara, 1983, p. 99).

Deciphered messages also betrayed Fujiwara's network to the FECB, which was aware of the four covert officers at the Singora consulate, four army and navy officers sent to the embassy in

Bangkok under assumed names, at least two saboteurs at large in Singapore, military communications specialists operating at several Japanese consulates in Thailand, and Tokyo's clandestine efforts to funnel money for espionage and subversion to its Bangkok embassy. Allied cryptanalysts also knew that the pro-Japanese Thai faction wanted Japan to maneuver Britain into becoming the aggressor[155] (Allen, 1991, p. 85; DoD, 1978, appx. IV, p. A-537). Special Branch detectives already had Ibrahim and Singapore's KAME cell under surveillance and realized that its members were spreading anti-British propaganda. Detectives arrested *Dōmei* reporter and KAME organizer Kaite Yoshi on December 5 as he was boarding a Thai steamer with a group of Japanese businessmen bound for Bangkok. A quick search of his luggage disclosed that Kaite was carrying KAME's detailed plans for an uprising to Fujiwara (1983, pp. 52, 99–100).

When news of the Japanese landings reached Singapore during the early morning hours of December 8, Special Branch police descended on *Warta Malaya*'s offices and caught KAME leaders in the midst of sending orders to cell members throughout Malaya to rise up and assist the Japanese invaders. All were arrested, including Ibrahim. Confiscated KAME membership lists and related documents implicated several more resident Japanese who were promptly interned. During the first three days of the war, security police arrested more than a hundred Malay members of KAME and confined them in the Changi Jail to await transport to prison in India (Kennard, 1947, p. 6; Lebra, 1977, pp. 13–114; Fujiwara, 1983, pp. 99–100, 318n20).

The arrests blunted the possibility of a nation-wide uprising, but some conspirators escaped the police dragnet. At a minimum,

KAME cells in Khota Baru guided Japanese landing barges ashore and led the invaders to British fighting positions (Fujiwara, 1983, pp. 99–100). KAME members at Ipoh showed trails through the undergrowth to Japanese units, cut telephone lines, and placed obstacles on roads to disrupt British communications. But no massive fifth column uprising disrupted British military operations and Malays provided little assistance to the invaders. Contemporary British counterintelligence assessments debunked many reports of espionage or sabotage as "unconfirmed" or "very unreliable" while postmortems exaggerated a fifth column's overall worth[156] (TNA, KV3/426, 100; Farrell, 2015, p. 720; Allen, 1991, pp. 254–255).

Aftermath

Following the British surrender of Singapore in mid-February 1942, the Japanese conquerors released Ibrahim and the other imprisoned Malay KMM leaders, replacing them in the cells with captured British officials. That June, however, Singapore's new Japanese rulers banned the KMM; evidence perhaps that the association's Malay nationalism superseded any loyalty to Japan (Lebra, 1977, p. 114). Shinozaki was also freed from prison and stayed on in various administrative positions during the Japanese occupation. Tsurumi returned as Governor of the Japanese-occupied Malacca Province. Toyoda returned to occupied Singapore in March 1942 and eventually became Director, General Affairs Department, Provisional City Government, for Shōnan (Singapore). In May 1946, during testimony to the U.S. Office of the Chief Counterintelligence Officer in Tokyo, he denied being a spy and testified that he had no knowledge of intelligence activities in the Singapore consulate during his tenure. Captain Heenan continued his treason by secretly transmitting intelligence to guide Japanese air raids in northern Malaya for several days after the Japanese invasion until he was finally caught red-handed. Court-martialed and imprisoned on the spot, he was later taken to Singapore where he was executed under circumstances that remain sketchy (Elphick and Smith, 1994, pp. 207, 216–217).

Police also rounded up all Japanese residents of Singapore in a series of early morning raids on December 8, 1941. Beginning around 2:00 a.m., bearded Sikh constables pounded on doors, awakening Japanese with orders to pack one small suitcase and come along. Decades of suspicion about Japanese fishermen culminated with the internment of Eifuku Tora and his family along with 475 fishermen, 329 of which were from Eifuku's company (Hiroshi and Hiroshi, 2002, pp. 119–120). Another internee was 31-year-old Ōmori Kichijirō, the last remaining executive of Senda and Company's rubber estate, suspected by police of money laundering, drug smuggling, and associating with known or alleged agents like Shinozaki, Eifuku, and so forth[157] (TNA, KV3/426, 52). They made no such allegations against Fukuda Kurahachi, a long-term Singapore resident and very successful businessman/merchant, but interred him anyway (de Matos and Ward, 2022, pp. 4–5).

Ōmori was taken to a nearby police station and, as more detainees like Fukuda arrived around noon, was moved to a warehouse near Keppel Harbor. That evening, about 150 Japanese men were herded onto a barge headed for Port Swettenham, where the detainees were held for two weeks under guard behind barbed wire in a derelict quarantine station. Japanese women and children were interned at a separate location. As the Japanese army approached nearby Kuala Lumpur, on Christmas night, guards packed the male detainees aboard a ship then returned them to Singapore and cells in Changi Jail. When the remorseless Japanese advance threatened Singapore in mid-January, all male detainees were shipped to Calcutta, India. Then followed a seventy-hour train ride to a desolate camp outside Delhi (Frei, 2004, pp. 7–8, 54–59; "Round-Up of Japanese," *Advocate* (Burnie, Tasmania), December 9, 1941, p. 5).

Detainees were housed six-to-a-tent under grim conditions at an old, abandoned fort. A week later wives and children arrived. The Japanese population eventually grew to about 2,000, about 90 of whom the British police listed as "suspect and dangerous." That September, about 700 detainees were exchanged for a like number of British civilians held in Singapore. Among those repatriated were Eifuku Tora and John Fujii, even though both were regarded as "suspect and dangerous." This is less surprising than it appears, because Japanese consuls from across the British empire in Asia, who were held under a more benign house arrest in India, nominated the internees for exchange. Fukuda was one of the fortunate ones selected (de Matos and Ward, 2022, pp. 17–18).

Other innocent Japanese civilians remained in the camp, enduring increasingly desperate circumstances. The flimsy tents offered little protection against winter cold or summer heat, and the Japanese government lodged a formal protest that the food, cooking, and sanitation facilities were inadequate. London refused to consider these allegations on the grounds that Japanese were "notoriously unable to cope with extremes of heat and cold." "According to Asiatic standards," Colonial Office bureaucrats observed, the rations were "adequate for proper nourishment." Middle class Japanese families of salaried workers and managers for trading companies, mining and rubber estates, and commercial enterprises fared poorly in such a harsh environment. Housewives and children suffered disproportionately. More than 100 died by the end of 1942, including 42 women and 9 children. For the comparable period, 29 European internees died in Changi Jail under Japanese captivity. At war's end, British authorities deported the surviving Japanese in India to Japan and also expelled all Japanese residents from British Malaya (Peter, 2007). In 1954, a few Japanese like Fukuda returned to Singapore after living under an Allied Occupation in defeated and devastated Japan where the Singapore Japanese were strangers.

Conclusions

The overall success of Singapore's spies during the interwar years is debatable. During the 1920s, the Japanese consulate worked with naval attachés to gather mainly open-source intelligence about the emerging Singapore naval base. During the 1930s, the consulate remained the pivot of Japanese intelligence gathering but expanded into espionage: illegal operations that involved the Japanese navy and prominent members of the resident Japanese community. By early 1940, the consulate had evolved to a center of intelligence collection, espionage, and sedition in Singapore, and it provided the support system for the Japanese staff officers who spied on Malaya in 1940 and 1941.

Japanese agents persistently spied on Singapore from the early 1920s. Diplomats, military and naval officers, businessmen, doctors, correspondents, fishermen, and blue-collar workers doubled as spies. Their methods and targets changed over time and their successes waxed and waned throughout the interwar period. During the early 1930s, reliance upon untrained "secret agents" dependent on an unreliable spy ring of resident Japanese may have ended in a fiasco, but it foreshadowed a more aggressive Japanese covert intelligence campaign, as the consulate was producing quality intelligence about the

Singapore naval base, aerial reinforcements, and improved air defenses by the later 1930s.

Individual Japanese companies in Malaya unquestionably offered aid and comfort to spies, from ISK providing agent cover identities to Eifuku Tora mounting motion picture cameras in the masts of his fishing trawlers. A handful of individual Japanese residents also abetted espionage, serving as guides, couriers, paymasters, recruiters, and so forth. They were normally businessmen planted in Japanese commercial enterprises, persons of wealth or status who exerted influence within the Japanese communities, or agents under the direction of the consulate, which coordinated their activities, collated their data, and transmitted intelligence reports to Tokyo. Few ordinary Japanese residents who lived hand-to-mouth directly engaged in espionage. Just a few months before the Japanese invasion, the American writer Martha Gellhorn aptly described Singapore's Japanese residents as "mostly poor people, who have a tendency to make themselves small and keep quiet" (Gellhorn, 1941, p. 43).

The larger homogenous ethnic group, almost all of whom sympathized with Japan's aims, was either ignorant of spies and agents operating in their midst or loath to expose them, or was willing to look the other way and indirectly support Tokyo's intelligence machinations to maintain harmony within the group. Japan's diplomatic and military intelligence networks relied on the social cohesiveness of the many residents of the close-knit Japanese communities across Singapore and Malaya to cloak the espionage of the few. The presence of actual Japanese spies embedded within the larger Japanese society made all Japanese suspect, more so as Japan itself seemed menacing (Everest-Phillips, 2007, p. 246).

The Japanese army staff officers who made firsthand assessments of the British defenses of Malaya and Singapore during 1940–1941 were the most successful spies. These professional soldiers either legally or clandestinely infiltrated Malaya. Senior consulate officials, select Japanese businessmen, and a handful of resident Japanese knew who they were and what they were doing. The consulate acted as a clearinghouse for their reports and transmitted them to Tokyo. Elite Japanese trading companies provided these spies with transportation and guides as well as their own operatives to gather information. Some long-time Japanese residents provided them necessities of food and lodging. The connections that Ōuchi had forged with rural Japanese communities during the 1930s unintentionally became the basis for informal support groups that facilitated, either deliberately or unwittingly, the army's espionage efforts. It was not reports from ordinary Japanese residents, but the ones from army officers that were beamed to Tokyo from the Singapore consulate that so impressed the FECB during 1941.

Earlier, Okubo's serial blunders had revealed to Special Branch the activities and key personalities of the active spy network run by resident Japanese in Singapore and their links to the consulate. Ineptitude on the consulate's part exposed a second potential spy ring following the outbreak of war in Europe in 1939. The loss of two spy networks within six years did not lessen the Singapore consulate's appetite for espionage, owing to the new consul-general's aggressive personality, the Foreign Ministry's new hard line, and Japan's steady drift toward war with the West.

Anglo-Japanese relations deteriorated rapidly during the early 1940s, spurring the consulate to extend its covert reach and use Malays in subversion and espionage roles. By mid-1941, the Singapore consulate was reporting the espionage successes and promoting internal subversion to support a Japanese invasion of Malaya. Ibrahim's Malay fifth column had very limited success as an indigenous espionage and sedition network but exerted disproportionate psychological effects by convincing the British military of widespread Malay treachery.

The Japanese community in Singapore was one of several ethnic neighborhoods—Chinese, Malay, Indian—that the special police constantly investigated in order to stifle communism, anti-British and anti-colonial sentiment, labor activism, and so on; in short, policing any perceived internal danger to the status quo. During much of this period, the counter-Japanese section operated on a niggardly budget that indicated its lack of importance or competence or both. Police leaders fluctuated between indifference to a Japanese threat and obsessive concern about Japanese designs.

The absence of an integrated counterintelligence agency encouraged backbiting between special branch and the military that hampered spy-catching. Discovery of the 1934 Okubo ring highlighted the chaotic state of Singapore's counterintelligence forces. Halfway measures to remedy the shortcomings were always short on money and long on irascible personalities. Singapore authorities did deport or imprison several Japanese on espionage charges but devised no comprehensive policy to deal with the internal menace. Special Branch repeatedly recommended mass detentions of Japanese residents that senior

Colonial Office authorities in London routinely rejected due to concern about Japanese retaliation against British residents in Japan or in Japanese-controlled territory. Nor was London willing to compromise its intelligence sources and services by acknowledging that British espionage had provided iron-clad proof of Japanese spying. Thus, authorities could not deport Ōuchi in 1938 nor close the Singapore consulate in 1941. The legal complexities and international repercussions of dealing with subversives nested in a minority ethnic community were never resolved and that enabled Singapore's spies to harvest useful intelligence until the eve of the Japanese invasion.

Regardless of bureaucratic in-fighting and financial and personnel limitations, the Special Police had successes. They had identified the Singapore Consulate as the linchpin of Japan's espionage operations. They knew which consul diplomats were intelligence operatives. They knew that privileged members within the expatriate Japanese community like Ōuchi Tsuneo or leading businessmen like Eifuku Tora were active in espionage operations. They were knowledgeable enough about the goings-on in the larger Japanese community to identify suspicious lowlifes as well as the skilled cadre of diplomats, business-owners, and professionals who directed espionage and subversion within Singapore. The Special Police did their job, and they were aware of the local situation. Nothing was done about it because previous police-created embarrassments caused military officers and Colonial Office bureaucrats to take police reports with a large dose of skepticism and often refuse to act on police-generated counterintelligence. Special police at all levels grated under the military's condescension and London's "soft" approach, naturally resenting the Services' or colonial authorities' caviler dismissal or indifference to their perspective. That stated, the police were often so focused on local internal matters that they failed to appreciate a larger more complex world beyond their precincts.

Legal and political considerations, organizational (administrative) failures, and wishful thinking hamstrung British counterintelligence efforts. The 1934 case opened a window on Japanese espionage in Singapore. London would not take advantage of the moment, insisting that the preservation of long-range secret sources outweighed any short-term gain. It also comported with a larger political–military strategy of not provoking Japan. As early as 1932, the British Chiefs of Staff acknowledged that they lacked the military forces to counter Japanese aggression. Nine years later, they still counseled against provoking Japan for the same reason.

Senior administrators in London and Singapore alike consistently underestimated the external Japanese danger and internal Malay nationalism because they substituted wishful thinking for British inability to meet commitments to a sprawling and vulnerable empire that they could no longer protect. Short-changing Singapore's defense included short-changing counterintelligence and enabled Singapore's spies to provide Tokyo with valuable intelligence as Japanese espionage and subversion spread throughout the colony.

Notes

1. Letter, Mr. G. S. Delmar Morgan to the Superintendent, C. I. D. Bombay, 15 Jun 1942. Morgan was describing Kuala Lumpur society, but the observation is pertinent to Singapore as well.

2. According to Wigmore, Chinese made up 43 per cent of the population, Indians 14 per cent, and Malays 41 per cent.

3. D. S. O. Singapore, "Encloses report on general security position in Malaya up to 31.3.41," 22 Apr 1941.

4. War Cabinet 616 A, "Draft conclusions of a meeting held at 10 Downing Street, SW1, on Friday, August 15 1919 at 11:30 a.m."

5. Zai Ei tōkumei zenken taishi (Matsudaira) e Gaimudaijin (Shidehara), "Shingapōru konkyochi ni kansuru hen," Shōwa go nen shichi gatsu tōka, (Cable, Ambassador London to Foreign Minister, matters related to the Singapore base, 10 Jul 1930).

6. Zai Shingapōru sōryōji dairi (Itō) e Gaimudaijin (Shidehara), "Chiyangi bōei setsubi chūshi no kansuru shimbun kirinuki sōfu no hen," Shōwa rokunen yongatsu tōka, (Cable, Acting Singapore Consul General (Itō) to Foreign Minister (Shidehara), matters of forwarding newspaper clippings related to the suspension of construction of the Changi defensive works, 10 Apr 1931).

7. "Imperial Defence Policy," Note by the Treasury on the Annual Review for 1932 by the Chiefs of Staff Sub-Committee (1082-B). Treasury Chambers, March 11, 1932, conclusions of a meeting of the Cabinet held at 10 Downing Street, SW1, on Wednesday, 23rd March 1932 at 11:00 a.m.

8. Zai Singapōru sōryōji – Gaimudaijin, "Tōchi rikugun butai idō hōkoku no hen, Shōwa kyūnen jūichigatsu nanoka" (Matters

related to the announcement of local army unit transfers), 7 Nov 1934.

9. Military Intelligence Officer's notes, "Japanese Espionage," 5 Dec 1934; letter, S. A. H. Kirkby, D. O. HQ, Malaya Command, to LTC Grimsdale, R. E., G. S., War Office, 13 Dec 1934.

10. "Notes of an inquiry held under Section 4(i) of Ordinance 153 (banishment) in the Singapore Civil Prison on the 14th and 15th January 1935."

11. Letter, Kirkby to Grimsdale, 13 Dec 1934.

12. Military Intelligence Officer's notes, "Japanese Espionage," 5 Dec 1934.

13. Special Branch, Straits Settlement Police, "An account of the visit of two Japanese secret service agents to Singapore November–December, 1934," Appendix No. 1 Japanese diary, 31 Jan 1935.

14. Letter, Governor-General Straits Settlements to the Secretary of State for the Colonies, 21 Dec 1934, with attachment "synopsis of events and information relative to local Japanese political activities and espionage, recorded as observed of received at the time and subject to revision in view of later information." Hereafter "Synopsis of local Japanese espionage."

15. Appendix S[pecial]. B[ranch]. Japanese diary, 30 September 1934, "Visit to the South Seas of a party of Japanese sea scouts in sailing brigantine the 'Giyu *Wani* Maru.'" The *Wani* Maru carried a large number of navy technicians because they were testing radio transmission frequencies and reception during the voyage.

16. A deciphered cable from the Japanese consul-general Singapore to the Foreign Ministry in Tokyo dated 10 December 1934 provided this *ex post facto* intelligence. See message, R.N.O. Shanghai to C-in-C, China, "reference Singapore espionage case," 20 Jan 1934 [sic].

17. "Synopsis of local Japanese espionage."

18. "Synopsis of local Japanese espionage."

19. Note A. D. S. B. (Assistant Director Special Branch) to D. D. S. (Deputy Director Security), 8 Apr 1935 and letter, Naval Intelligence Centre, Fort Canning, Singapore to DNI Rear Admiral G. C. Dickens, 3 Mar 1935.

20. Letter, Naval Intelligence Officer Singapore to Admiral Dickens, 25 Dec 1934; "Notes for Captain Waller," 12 Dec 1934.

21. "Notes for Captain Waller;" letter, Naval Intelligence Officer to Dickens, 25 Dec 1934.

22. "Synopsis of local Japanese espionage."

23. "Military Intelligence Officer's notes," 5 Dec 1934; letter, Kirkby to Grimsdale, 31 Jan 1935.

24. Telegram, Governor of the Straits Settlements to the Secretary of State for Colonies, 8 December 1934; "Synopsis of local Japanese espionage;" "Military Intelligence Officer's notes," 5 Dec 1934.

25. Telegram, General, Singapore to A. S. D. (B.) (Harold Steptoe, Secret Intelligence Service representative in Shanghai, China), 7 Dec 1934.

26. Telegram, Governor to Secretary State Colonies, 8 Dec 1934; telegram, G. O. C. Malaya to the War Office, 10 Dec 1934; letter, Governor Straits Settlement to the Secretary of State for Colonies, 21 Dec 1934, with enclosure, H. Fairburn. I. G. P., "Further report on the Japanese espionage case," 20 Dec 1934; "Account of visit of two Japanese secret service agents to Singapore," Appendix No. 1, Japanese diary, 31 Jan 1935.

27. Special Branch police received several reports that an important third man was coming either from India or Siam but was unable to account for such a person. Letter, Kirkby to Grimsdale, 13 Dec 1934 and "Synopsis of local Japanese espionage." Siam was the nation's official name until 24 June 1939 when it was changed to Thailand. The name reverted after the Second World War but on 11 May 1949 again became Thailand. See Reynolds, 1994, p. 28 on the political implications of the name change.

28. Letter, Kirkby to Grimsdale, 6 Dec 1934 with enclosure, "Further report on the Japanese espionage case;" "Synopsis of local Japanese espionage."

29. Letter, Kirkby to Grimsdale, 31 Jan 1935, "Synopsis of local Japanese espionage;" Military Intelligence Officer's notes, 5 Dec 1934; letter, Kirkby to Grimsdale, 6 Dec 1934; "Further report on Japanese espionage case."

30. "Further report on Japanese espionage case." For the RAF warrant officer's statement describing Ohki's entrapment see "Notes of an inquiry under Section 4(1) of Ordinance No. 153 (banishment) relation to an application by the police that S. Ohki, Japanese be banned from the colony," 29 Jan 1935.

31. Telegram, Governor to Secretary of State for the Colonies," 8 Dec 1934; D.O. Singapore to G. S., W. O., 13 Dec 1934; "Further report on Japanese espionage case;" Naval Intelligence Officer, Singapore, "Comments on Military Intelligence Officer's notes." Kokubo was banished effective 12 March 1935.

32. "Military Intelligence Officer's notes," 5 Dec 1934; telegram (paraphrase), Special Branch, police, Singapore to Shanghai (Steptoe), 7 Dec 1934.

33. Telegram, Governor to Secretary of State for Colonies, 8 Dec 1934; "Military Intelligence Officer's notes," 5 Dec 1934.

34. Letter, Kirkby to Grimsdale, 13 Dec 1934; telegram, G. O. C. Malaya to the War Office, 10 Dec 1934; telegram, Governor of the Straits Settlements to the Secretary of State for the colonies, 12 Dec 1934.

35. Shenton Thomas had arrived in Singapore on 9 November 1934.

36. Kirkby to Grimsdale, 13 Dec 1934; G. O. C. Malaya to War Office, 10 Dec 1934; telegram, Commodore, Singapore to C. in C. China, repeated Admiralty, 5 Dec 1934. Special Branch did request SIS tap the ship's wireless transmissions. Telegram, Special Branch to A. S. D. (B.), Steptoe, 7 Dec 1934; letter Naval Intelligence Officer to Admiral Dickens, 25 Dec 1934.

37. Letter, Singapore naval officer to LTC Forster, Admiralty, 9 Jan 1935, with attachment, "Japanese espionage;" letter, Naval Intelligence Centre, Singapore to DNI Dickens; "Account of visit of two Japanese secret service agents to Singapore," Appendix No. 1, Japanese diary, 31 Jan 1935.

38. "Japanese espionage;" letter, Kirkby to Grimsdale, 31 Jan 1935; "Military Intelligence Officer's notes," 5 Dec 1934.

39. From SIS – "connection between Semphill and Kaseda," 18 Dec 1934. The cable's originator and recipient are blocked out and it is unclear how SIS obtained the cable.

40. ST, "Prominent Singapore Japanese falls dead in police office," ST, "Allegations of spying?;" "Singapore espionage," *The Argus*, Melbourne, VC, Aus., 11 Dec 1934, p. 9.

41. "Death of Mr. Nishimura." The Japan Association became the Japan Society after the Second World War.

42. "Summaries regarding suspect and dangerous Japanese interned," Apr 1942.

43. Telegram, Governor to Secretary of State for the Colonies, 8 Dec 1934; telegram, Governor General of the Straits Settlements to the Secretary of State for the Colonies, 10 Dec 1934; telegram, the Secretary of State for the Colonies to Governor of the Straits Settlements, 10 Dec 1934. These last comments applied to preliminary talks preceding the Second London Naval Conference set for 1936. By late 1934, Tokyo had already decided to abandon naval limitations treaties. Sadao Asada, 2007, pp. 149–150; Pelz, 1974, p. 132.

44. Telegram, Governor to Secretary State for Colonies, 10 Dec 1934.

45. Telegram, R.N.O. Shanghai to C-in-C, China, "Reference Singapore espionage case," 20 Jan 1934 [sic].

46. On the role of Japanese commercial firms see Memo, M.O.2. to various, 27 May 1942 with enclosure "Espionage through business."

47. Letter, British Naval Attaché, Tokyo to Aide de Camp, Navy Minister, Captain Tayui Jō, 14 Jan 1935.

48. For example: Telegram, Tokumei zenken kōshi, (Minister plenipotentiary Siam [Yatabe Tatsukichi]) to Gaimudaijin, (foreign minister), 29 Mar 1935.

49. A retired Imperial Navy officer established the *Shinsei Ryūjinkai* in November 1934. Although tiny, about 50–60 members, it attracted Japanese aristocrats, a member of the House of Peers, a retired army colonel, and Kaseda among its members. *Shinsei Ryūjinkai* described a mystic, millennial theocracy that required the reconciliation of the unbroken imperial line with a spiritual imperial genealogy that included evil deities. Citing flagrant disrespect as grounds for lèse majeste, police arrested several members, and the *Shinsei Ryūjinkai* disbanded in March 1936. Tsushima, 2000, Part 2.

50. Memo, M.O.2 for M.S. 1 et al., M.O.2/BU/2140, 27 May 1942, with enclosure "Extracts of reports on the Malayan campaign."

51. Note, A. D. S. B. to D. D. S., 8 Apr 1935.

52. Letter, Sir Eric Holt-Wilson, Deputy Director, MI-5 to DNI (Rear-Admiral G. C. Dickens), 12 Apr 1935 and letter, Naval Intelligence Centre to DNI, 3 Mar 1935. Wynne remained in Straits Settlements Police, eventually rising to Deputy Inspector General by 1941. Ban, 2001, p. 136.

53. Letters, B. Herdman to H. P. Bryson, 28 Mar and 11 Apr 1972. Mrs. Herdman (née Brown) was Morgan's private secretary in the Japanese section.

54. Letter, Herdman to Bryson, 11 Apr 1972, Civilian internment.

55. According to Mrs. Herdman, "Bell was absolute anathema to Morgan." Letter, Herdman to Bryson, 28 Mar 1972. It should be remembered that after Singapore's fall Morgan survived almost four years in Japanese internment, including an initial period of prolonged solitary confinement. Bell left Singapore before the war with Japan and died in London, England, in April 1944.

56. Letter, Bryson to Herdman, 8 Apr 1972.

57. Letter, F. Hayley Bell to Sir Vernon [Kell], 30 Apr 1937.

58. W. Ormsby Gore, Downing Street to Governor Straits Settlements, 19 Feb 1938; Under Secretary of State, Foreign Office C. W. Orde to the Under Secretary of State Colonial Office, G. E. J. Gent, Esq., 1 Feb 1938; draft letter, Gore to Governor Straits Settlement, 19 Feb 1938, quote. The quoted material was excised from the final correspondence.

59. Letters, Gore to Governor Straits Settlements, 19 Feb 1938 and Orde to Gent, 10 Feb 1938.

60. Draft note, Gent to F. O., 17 Feb 1938.

61. Letter, Herdman to Bryson, 11 Apr 1972.

62. Major K. S. Morgan, Special Branch to Inspector-General of Police, 18 Jan 1939; Report "C," Detailed report on the raid on Ohara Tomoyoshi, Japan Trade Bureau, Japan Industrial Bureau," Appendix E, Secret letter No. 92, Kenji Kodama, President Foreign Trade Association, Tokyo to Asajiro Tate, Singapore Trade Agency, 27 Oct 1938 and Appendix F, letter, Tomokichi Ohara, Chief, Trade Recommendation Bureau, Singapore to Kenji Kodama, 9 Nov 1938.

63. Report "C," Appendix K, Secret letter No. 15, Ohara to Kodama, 16 Jan 1939.

64. Report "C," Appendix G, Letter, Ohara to Kodama, 9 Nov 1938.

65. K. S. Morgan, Report "A," "General report on the raids detailing the circumstances leading up to them. Information leading up to the raid," 4 Feb 1939.

66. Memo, K.S. Morgan to Inspector-General of Police, S. B., Singapore, 22 Dec 1938. Secret.

67. Report "A," "Information leading up to the raid."

68. Memo, K. S. Morgan, Special Branch, S. S. Police to Inspector-General of Police, S. S., 18 Jan 1939, Report "B." The fourth target was the Japanese-owned Pilot Pen Company.

69. Report "A," "Information leading up to the raid."

70. Memo L34, (?) to M.I. 5 (Mr. Robertson), 3 Apr 1939, Secret, with attachment, copy of dispatch dated 4.2.39 from [British] Consul-General, Batavia, NEI.

71. Report "B."

72. "Tokio diplomatic protest over Singapore incidents."

73. Marginalia, Director MI-5 (Kell) to B-3 (MI-5 Intelligence), 4 Mar 1939.

74. Letter, Office of the Director Special Branch (Bell) to Sir Vernon Kell (MI-5), 24 Mar 1939.

75. Letter, Herdman to Bryson, 28 Mar 1972.

76. "Note by Sir Arthur Jelf," 30 Jul 1942.

77. "Report of Messrs J. E. D. and B. H. D. Elias, Singapore," recorded 11 Mar 1942.

78. D. S. O. (Johnstone) Singapore to War Office, London, "Japanese espionage in Malaya," 26 Nov 1941.

79. D. S. O. Singapore, "Espionage," 15 Oct 1941; D. S. O. Singapore, "Encloses report on general security position in Malaya up to 31.3.41," 22 Apr 1941.

80. Gunreibu dai 3 bu (Naval general staff, 3rd department), "Eikoku kyōkutō saksen yōsō heiryoku," (Estimated English operational strength in the Far East): "Beppyō dai san, "Kyōkutō idō shi erubeki Eikugun seiryoku," (Statistical table no 3, British airpower that can be transferred to the Far East), Shōwa 13.12 (Dec 1938).

81. Imoto (1998, p. 62) describes his unofficial trip as the army's traditional long leave policy before an assignment in Europe and mentions in passing the intelligence collection aspect of his travel. According to Yamamoto (2016, p. 303, n166), Imoto omitted a lengthy (110 page) account of his Malaya mission from his original manuscript before publication.

82. Gunreibu dai sanbu, "Hitō, Honkon, Shingaka hōmen no jōsei" (Conditions in the areas of the Philippines, Hong Kong, and Singapore) 9–4-14, 4 Sep 1939.

83. Extract, "Removal of potential enemy subjects from vital areas, etc.," 1942; first quote: D. S. O. Singapore, 22 Apr 1941, encloses "Report on general security position in Malaya up to 31.3.41; second quote: "Minutes of the 17th meeting of the Defence Security Committee held on 11th November 1941, 13 Nov 41."

84. Extract, "Removal of potential enemy subjects from vital areas."

85. D. S. O. Singapore, 8 Jan 1941. Question mark in original.

86. H. Q. Malaya Command, "Extract encloses report of the general security position in Malaya up to 30.4.40," 11 Jul 1940.

87. Tanemura was a mid-grade staff officer assigned to the War Guidance Center, where he prepared the confidential war diary. Entries for 10 May and 22 Jun 1940, respectively.

88. "Summaries regarding suspect and dangerous Japanese interned," April 1942, Hirota Toku and Watanabe Toru.

89. For example, see Rikugun sanbō honbu, (Army general staff), "*Shingaka kaigun konkyochi shisetsu yōzu*," (Sketch maps of the Singapore naval base facilities), 13 Aug 1941.

90. The confidential war diary noted that Okada and LTC Shimamura Noriyasu likewise "had a sudden turn of attitude about the southern operation" (Gunjishi gakkai (eds.), 1998, p. 25, entry for 10 Sep 1940).

91. "Conclusions of a meeting of the War Cabinet held at 1 August 1940," 1 Aug 1940.

92. D. S. O., Singapore, 15 Oct 1940, "Extract of S.S. Police-Special Branch report upon current Japanese affairs, new series, dated 1.10.40;""Arrests of Japanese in Singapore."

93. Long-term, undercover army intelligence officers like Tamura had spent years in the Philippines, but perhaps the best known was Captain Maeda Masaji who from May 1924 through December 1928 posed as an employee for the Kimura Trading Company (Kimura *kaisha*), managing a laundry on Bataan. In December 1941, Major General Maeda

returned the Philippines as the chief of staff, Fourteenth Army. Hata et al. (eds.), 1963, pp. 176 and 391n5. Sugita was a Nanpō staff officer.

94. D. S. O. Singapore, "Sabotage and espionage," 1 Aug 1941.

95. "Japanese charged under secrets' ordinance" and "Trial of Japanese on secrets charges."

96. D. S. O. Singapore, "Sabotage and espionage," 1 Aug 1941.

97. D. S. O. Singapore, "Sabotage and espionage," 1 Aug 1941.

98. D. S. O. Singapore, "Sabotage and espionage," 1 Aug 1941.

99. "Japanese charged," and "Shinozaki convicted on two secrets charges." Under defence regulations a detainee in special police custody did not face jail or prison confinement until charges were announced.

100. D. S. O. Singapore, "Sabotage and espionage," 1 Aug 1941.

101. "Police evidence at Shinozaki trial" and "Shinozaki convicted." Yamakawa was not recalled and lived in Singapore until her deportation to India in 1942.

102. The envelope contained two letters, one Shinozaki's maudlin message in case of his detention and the other an attempt to dispel any suspicions about Yamakawa Kamenosuke, a proofreader at the Singapore *Nippō*, Atusko's father, and suspected by police as a long-term spy. Toyoda served as consul general from September 13 1939 to Nov 2 1940.

103. D. S. O. Singapore, 15 Oct 1940, "Extract from S.S. Police report upon current Japanese affairs new series, dated 10 January 1940 [sic],""Arrests of Japanese in Singapore;" D. S. O. Singapore, 8 Jan 1941, "Extract from S.S. Police 'report upon current Japanese affairs dated 31st December 1940;""Arrests of Japanese in Malaya."

104. D. S. O. Singapore, 8 Jan 1941, "Extract from S.S. Police report upon current Japanese affairs," dated 31st December 1940, "Arrests of Japanese in Malaya."

105. D. S. O. Singapore, 8 Jan 1941, "Arrests of Japanese in Malaya."

106. Toyoda returned to occupied Singapore in March 1942 and eventually became Director, General Affairs Department, Provisional City Government for Shōnan (Singapore). In May 1946, during testimony to the U.S. Office of the Chief Counter-Intelligence Officer in Tokyo, he denied being a spy and testified that he had no knowledge of intelligence activities in the Singapore consulate during his tenure.

107. D. S. O. Singapore, 22 Apr 1941, encloses report on general security position in Malaya up to 31.3.41.

108. D. S. O. Singapore, 22 Apr 1941, report on general security position in Malaya up to 31.3.41.

109. War Cabinet, Chiefs of Staff Committee, report, "Implications of Japanese penetration of Indo-China and Thailand," C.O.S. (40) 905, 6 Nov 1940.

110. "*Jūnigatsu nijūshichinichi dai sankai renraku kondankai*" (Third liaison roundtable discussion), 27 Dec 1940.

111. For a differing version see Yamamoto (2016, p. 276) who, based on the official Japanese war history, writes that Kunitake entered British Malaya disguised as a member of the Japanese consulate.

112. D. S. O. Singapore, dated 15.10.41, "Espionage."

113. D. S. O. Singapore, 5 Aug 1941, "Report on general security position in Malaya up to 31.6.41."

114. The two were Nomura Mamoru and Toyoshima Tokusaburō. "Summaries regarding suspect and dangerous Japanese interned."

115. Extract "Removal of potential enemy subjects from vital areas, etc.," not dated but likely early 1942.

116. "Veteran units join Singapore defense" and "Large new force is landed at Singapore: Men and machines for Malay defense: More troops land in Singapore area."

117. "Singapore is reinforced."

118. Telegram, Tokyo to Hsinking, #693, 13 Oct 1941; retransmits Singapore to Tokyo #630, 9 Oct 1941. [Accessed February 26, 2017.]

119. Telegram, Tokyo to Singapore, 22 Oct 1941 [Accessed February 26, 2017.]

120. *Odd Man Out* offers the only book-length treatment of Heenan.

121. Heenan's treason appears briefly in the following documents: D. S. O. Singapore, "Espionage and fifth column," 20 Jan 1942, 102; Letter to Sir Arthur Jelf, 23 Dec 1942 with attachment, statement, G. S. Delmar Morgan to the Superintendent C. I. D. Bombay, 15 Jun 1942, 67; "Extract from Malaya and Singapore: Report drawn up by Major H. B. Thomas, CBE, IA," circa July 1942, 74, identified a "European" detected using a secret transmitter.

122. D. S. O. Singapore, "Report on general security position in Malaya up to 31 – 6 41," 5 Aug 1941.

123. Telegram C. in C. China to Admiralty, 14 Jun 1941.

124. D. S. O. Singapore, "Espionage," 15 Oct 1941.

125. Director, FECB, "Report on an investigation of special intelligence reports concerning Japanese espionage activities in Malaya," 4 Nov 1941.

126. Director, FECB, "Report on an investigation of special intelligence reports concerning Japanese espionage activities in Malaya," 4 Nov 1941.

127. C. in C. China to Admiralty, 14 Jun 1941 and D. S.O. Singapore, "Espionage and fifth column," 20 Jan 1942. The Royal Corps of Signals complained about the lack of cooperation with Posts and Telegraphs Department of Malaya.

128. Note by Sir Arthur Jelf, 30 Jul 1942.

129. D. S. O. Singapore, "Espionage," 15 Oct 1941 and letter, D. S. O. Singapore to War Office, London, "Japanese espionage in Malaya," 26 Nov 41.

130. D. S. O. Singapore to War Office, "Japanese espionage," 26 Nov 41; note by Sir Arthur Jelf, 30 Jul 1942.

131. Sanbō honbu (Headquarters army general staff), "Eiryō Marai jōhō kiroku" (English occupied Malaya intelligence records), "Marai gumbi" dai 1, "heiryoku" (Part 1 Malaya military armaments (1) troop strengths), Shōwa 16. 9. 20 (20 Sep 1941). Hereafter Sanbō honbu, Marai gumbi.

132. Gunreibu, "Hitō EiryōMarai oyobi Ran-In," 1941.

133. Sanbō honbu, "Marai gumbi," (3) "Eiryō Mare jōrikuten" (Landing points in English occupied Malaya), Shōwa 16. 9. 20 (20 Sep 1941).

134. Sanbō honbu, "Marai gumbi," (3) "Eiryō Mare hikojō ichiranzu" (Catalogue of airfields in Englsh occupied Malaya), Shōwa 16. 9. 20 (20 Sep 1941).

135. Sanbō honbu, "Marai gumbi" (1) "heiryoku."

136. Gunreibu, "Hitō Eiryō Marai oyobi Ran-In," 1941.

137. In military terminology a flying column was a small unit that relied on rapid mobility and surprise to swiftly seize objectives.

138. Sanbō honbu, "Marai gunbi," (3) Eiryō Marai dōro dai ichi dōromō" (Roads in English occupied Malaya, part 1, road networks), Shōwa 16. 9. 20 (20 Sep 1941).

139. Sanbō honbu, "Marai gumbi," (3) "Eiryō Marai tetsudō dai ichi Marai tetsudō no nōryoku" (Railroads in English occupied Malaya, part 1, capacities of Malayan railroads), Shōwa 16. 9. 20 (20 Sep 1941).

140. Sanbō honbu, "Marai gumbi," (3) "Eiryō Marai tetsudō dai ichi Marai tetsudō no nōryoku."

141. Sanbō honbu, "Marai gumbi," (3) "Eiryō Mare ni okeru 'jyanguru' no jōkyō," ("Jungle" conditions in English occupied Malaya), Shōwa 16. 9. 20 (20 Sep 1941).

142. Tsuji perpetrated the coolie story in his highly embellished postwar account that further sensationalized Asaeda's

exploits, which, while important, were far less dramatic (Tsuji, 1993, pp. 7, 24–25). For a sensationalized account of Asaeda's exploits see Farago, 1967, pp. 121–122.

143. The Guards Division was in French Indochina, the Takumi Detachment in Guangzhou, the 5th Division in Shanghai, and the 18th Division on Taiwan. The senior officers in turn passed the documents to subordinate officers to study while aboard the troop transports carrying them to the invasion beaches.

144. Harimau of Malaya was the pseudonym for Tani Yutaka, the son of a Japanese barber living in the east coast town of Kuala Trengganu. During Chinese protests over Japanese aggression in China during 1932, Tani's six-year-old sister was kidnapped and murdered. Tani later formed a bandit gang active in southern Thailand and northern Malaya.

145. "Summaries regarding suspect and dangerous Japanese interned," John Tatsuki Fujii.

146. "Summaries regarding suspect and dangerous Japanese interned," Ishikawa Kaishu, Nago Shohei, Watanabe Itaru.

147. There are differing accounts of how the two men met. One claims Ibrahim contacted Ishiwara (mining engineer) offering his services to the Japanese. Another claims that Kaite acted as the intermediary and introduced the two. The two are not necessarily exclusive.

148. "Report of Messrs J. E. D. and B. H. D. Elias, Singapore," recorded 11 Mar 1942; D. S. O. Singapore, 20 Jan 1942, "Malay-Japanese fifth column organisation."

149. Report of Messrs Elias.

150. M. O. 2 to M. 5. 1 et al., encloses extracts from reports on Malayan Campaign, 27 May 1942, "Fifth column."

151. Report of Messrs Elias; D. S. O. Singapore, "Malay-Japanese fifth column organisation," 20 Jan 1942; "Summaries regarding suspect and dangerous Japanese interned," Kaite Takabashi.

152. "Summaries regarding suspect and dangerous Japanese interned," Kaite Takabashi.

153. Letter, Morgan to Superintendent, C. I. D. Bombay, 15 Jun 1942.

154. Note by Sir Arthur Jelf, 30 Jul 1942.

155. Telegram, Japanese ambassador Bangkok to Tokyo, #872, 29 Nov 1941. [Accessed May 17, 2022.]

156. Letter, D. S. O., Colombo to His Excellency the Governor, Colombo, 18 Feb 1942.

157. "Summaries regarding suspect and dangerous Japanese interned," Ohmori Kichiro [sic].

Suggested projects and discussion topics

- Was there an alternative to a naval base at Singapore?
- Did the Japanese cultural practice of apartness make them a natural target of British colonial police in the late 1920s and the 1930s?
- How did the Japanese government manipulate Japanese residents of Malaya?
- Why were Malays sympathetic toward Japan?
- Was there a unified British colonial policy in Singapore and London?
- Comment on internment/deportation of Japanese residents of Malaya following Japan's invasion of Malaya.

References

Allen, L. (1991) *Singapore, 1941–1942*. 2nd ed. London: Gainsborough House.

Asada, S. (2007) *Culture Shock and Japanese-American Relations: Historical Essays*. Columbia, MO: University of Missouri Press.

Asaeda, S. (1983) Interview by Handō Kazutoshi, "*Eikoku shijō saidai no kōfuku*," (The greatest surrender in English history) *Rekishi to jimbutsu*, pp. 114–127.

Aurora (2012) "Lord Semphill – Japanese spy?" www.kbismarck. org, naval history forums, 8 November. Available at: www.kbisma rck.org/forum/viewtopic.php?t=5609 [Accessed July 4, 2017].

Ban, K. C. (2001) *Absent History: The Untold Story of Special Branch Operations in Singapore, 1915–1942*. Singapore: Raffles edn.

BBKS (1984) Bōeichō bōei kenshūjō senshibu, (ed.), (1984) "Kisō chōsa 'Nihon rikukaigun no jōhō kikō to sono katsudō'" (Primary research-"Japan's army's and navy's intelligence structure and activities), Kenkyū shiryō 84RO-2H, mimeo.

BBKS (1985) Bōeichō, bōei kenshūjō, senshibu, (ed.), (1985) "Nanpō sakusen ni ōzuru rikugun no kyōiku kunren," (Army education and training to comply with the Southern operation), Kenkyū shiryō (research document) 85RO-3H, mimeo.

Best, A. (2002) *British Intelligence and the Japanese Challenge in Asia, 1914–1941*. New York: Palgrave MacMillian.

Bridges, B. (1986) "Britain and Japanese espionage in pre-war Malaya: The Shinozaki case," *Journal of Contemporary History*, 21(1), pp. 23–35.

"Brits in '34 feared Japan used Sea Scouts to mask espionage," Japan Times, 6 March 2006. Available at: www.japantimes.co.jp/ news/2006/03/06/national/brits-in-34-feared-japan-used-sea-scouts-to-mask-espionage [Accessed 5 July 2022].

Callahan, R. (1974) "The illusion of security: Singapore 1919–42," *Journal of Contemporary History*, 9(2): pp. 69–92.

Chua, A. and Seng, T. L. "Mamoru Shinozaki," Available at: Singapore Infopedia, National Library Board: eresources.nlb.gov. sg/infopedia/articles/SIP_1686_2010-07-26.html [Accessed 25 Oct 2017].

Coxy, F. (2009) Post no. 3: "RE: Colonel Francis Hayley Bell, internal security," Axis History Forum, 7 December. Available at: forum. axishistory.com/viewtopic.php?t=152391 [Accessed 3 July 2022].

CUDL (Cambridge University Digital Library) Cambridge University notes, Civilian internment: Notes on the Second World War: RCMS 103/12/26, v1, Available at: cudl.lib.cam.ac.uk/views/ MS-RCM-00103-00012-00026 [Accessed 23 May 2019].

de Matos, C. and Ward, R. (2022) "Forgotten forced migrants of war: Civilian Internment of Japanese in British India, 1941–6": pp. 1–29. Available at: researchonline.nd.edu.au/arts_article [Accessed 20 June 2022].

"Death of Mr. Nishimura,"The Singapore Free Press and Mercantile Advertiser, 7 December 1934. Available at: eresources.nlb.gov.sg/ newspapers/Digitised/Article/singfreepressb19341207-1.2.33. [3]. [Accessed 10 March 2017].

DesRoisers, E. (1966) "The Royal Navy, 1922–1930: The search for a naval policy in an age of re-adjustment." MA. McGill University. Available at: escholarship.mcgill.ca/concern/theses/w0892c334 [Accessed 21 May 2022].

DoD (Department of Defense, USA) (1978) "The 'Magic' background of Pearl Harbor, vol. 5." Available at: ibiblio.org/pha/ magic/vol-5html [Accessed 10 May 2022].

———. "The 'magic' background of Pearl Harbor, vol. 3, appendix 3." Available at: ibiblio.org/pha/magic/vol-3-app.html [Accessed May 10, 2022].

———. "The 'magic' background of Pearl Harbor, vol. 4, appendix 4." Available at: ibiblio.org/pha/magic/vol-4-app.html ibiblio.org/pha/magic/vol-4-app.html [Accessed May 17, 2022].

Elphick, P. and Smith, M. (1994) *Odd Man Out*. London: Hodder &Stoughton, Ltd., Coronet paperback edn.

Evans, D. C. and Peattie, M. R. (1997) *Kaigun: Strategy, Tactics, and Technology in the Imperial Japanese Navy 1887–1941*. Annapolis, MD: Naval Institute Press.

Everest-Phillips, M. (2007) "The Pre-war Fear of Japanese espionage: Its impact and legacy," *Journal of Contemporary History,* 42(2), pp. 243–265.

Farago, L. (1967) *The Broken Seal: "Operation Magic" and the Secret Road to Pearl Harbor*. New York: Random House.

Farrell, B. P. (2015) *The Defence and Fall of Singapore.* Singapore: Monsoon Books Pte Ltd.

Frei, H. (2004) *Guns of February: Ordinary Japanese Soldiers' Views of the Malayan Campaign & the Fall of Singapore 1941–1942*. Singapore: Singapore University Press.

Fujiwara, I. (1983) *F. Kikan: Japanese Army Intelligence Operations in Southeast Asia during World War II*, trans. by Akashi Yoji. Hong Kong: Heinemann Asia, edn.

Gellhorn, M. (1941) "Singapore Scenario: The Melodrama that may become and epic," *Collier's Weekly*, (August 9, 1941), pp. 20–21, 43–44. Available at unz.com/print/Colliers-1941aug09-00020/Contents/ [Accessed 2 June 2022].

Goodman, G. K. (2000) "Manila in June 1943," *Philippine Studies,* 48(3): pp. 415–419. Available at: jstor.org/stable/42634414 [Accessed 4 July 2022].

Gunjishi gakkai (eds.) (1998) *Daihon'ei rikugunbu sensō shidō han*, (Imperial general headquarters army department war guidance section) Kimitsu sensō nisshi, jō (Confidential war diary, vol. 1). Tokyo: Kinseisha.

Hanyok, R. J. (2008) *Cryptology and the Winds Message Controversy*. Collingdale, PA: DIANE Publishing.

Hata, I. et al. (eds.) (1963) *Taiheiyō sensō e no michi* (The road to the Pacific war): (6). Tokyo: Asahi Shimbunsha.

Hata I. (ed.) (1991) *Nihon rikukaigun sōgō jiten* (Composite dictionary of Japan's army and navy). Tokyo: Tokyo daigaku shuppankai.

Hiroshi, H. and Hiroshi, S. (2002) *Japan and Singapore in the World Economy: Japan's Economic Advance into Singapore 1870–1965*. London: Routledge.

History, S. G. (2014) "British restrict Japanese fishing in Singapore, Feb 1937": Available at: eresources.nlb.gov.sg/history/events/82be0a34-1076-4735-9aa7-19358dfa4bfe [Accessed 28 October 2017].

Imoto, K. (1998) *DaitōA sensō sakusen nisshi*, (Operations diary of the greater East Asian war). Fuyō shobō shuppan, rev ed.

"Japanese detained" Malaya Tribune, 5 Aug 1940, 1. Available at: eresources.nlb.gov.sg/newspapers/Digitised/Article/maltribune 19400805-1.2.35 [Accessed: 25 Mar 2017].

"Japanese released, at Singapore" *Cairns Post* (QLD: 1909-1954), 23 Sep 1940. Available at: trove.nia.gov.au/newspaperarticle/42255129? [Accessed: 25 March, 2017].

JCAR (Japan Center for Asian Historical Records). Available at: www.jacar.archives.go.jp

Kennard, A. (1947) "Jap fifth column in Malaya was small," *Straits Times*, 24 Aug 1947. Available at: eresources.nlb.gov.sg/newspapers/Digitised/Article/straitstimes19470824-1.2.57 [Accessed 15 May 2017].

Kennedy, G. (2010) "Anglo-American strategic relations and intelligence assessments of Japanese air power 1934–1941," *The Journal of Military History,* 74(3), pp. 737–773.

Koh, D. S. J. and Tanaka, K. (1984) "Japanese competition in the trade of Malaya in the 1930s," *Southeast Asian Studies* (March), 21(4), pp. 374–399.

Kunitake, T. (1988) "Mare-gun shireibu," (Malaya army headquarters) *Bessatsu Maru, Taiheiyō sensō shōgen shiri-zu,* 8, (Pacific war testimonies' series, 8) *Senshō no nichinichi,* (Daily military victories), pp. 462–495.

Kuwada, E. (1996) "Hikari kikan," (The Hikari agency) in Dōdai kurabu kōenshu, (1996) Dōdai keizai konwakai, eds., *Shōwa gunji hiwa, chū,* (Confidential tales of the Showa military, vol. 2) Dōdai keizai konwakai, pp. 223–254.

Lam, P. F. (2012) Whatever happens to the pre-war Japanese community in Singapore, [Blog], *lampfoo.com.* Available at: lampinfoo.com/2012/12/31/whatever-happens-to-the-pre-war-japanese-community-in-singapore [Accessed 1 June 2017].

Lebra, J. C. (1977) *Japanese-Trained Armies in Southeast Asia.* New York: Columbia University Press.

Liew, K. K. (2006) "Labour formation, identity, and resistance in HM Dockyard, Singapore (1921–1971), *International Review of Social History,* 51(3), pp. 415–439. Available at: academia.edu [Accessed 8 March 2017].

Maurice-Jones, COL K. W. (2012) *The History of Coast Artillery in the British Army,* Andrews UK Limited.

McCormick, A. H. (2006) "The volunteer forces of the federated and unfederated States of Malaya, and the Straits Settlements: 1940–1942; Summary" Available at: malayanvolunteersgroup.org.uk/node/58 [Accessed 9 March 2017].

Mercado, S. (2002) *The Shadow Warriors of Nakano.* Dulles, VA: Brassey's.

NEIG (Netherlands East Indies Government) (1942) *Ten Years of Japanese Burrowing in the Netherlands East Indies: Official Report of the on Japanese Subversive Activities in the Archipelago During the Last Decade.* New York: The Netherlands Information Bureau.

NSA (National Security Agency, USA), Center for Cryptologic History, United States Cryptologic History, Series IV, World War II, Volume 8, Robert L. Benson, *The Origin of U.S.-British Communications Intelligence Cooperation (1940-41).*

NYT (New York *Times*) Available at: www.proquest.com/hnp/newyorktimes/ [Accessed 11 July 2022].

Ōuchi, T. (1943) "Ōuchi Tsune cho 'Nantō ki' mokuji," (Table of contents for Ouchi Tsune's work "Record of the South Islands"). Nanyō keizai kenkyūkai.

Peattie, M. R. (1996) "Nanshin: The 'Southward Advance,' 1931–1941, as a prelude to the Japanese occupation of southeast Asia" in Peter Duus, Ramon H. Myers, and Mark R. Peattie eds., *The Japanese Wartime Empire, 1931–1945* (Princeton, NJ: Princeton University Press, 1996), pp. 189–242.

Peter, H. (2007) "Interned Japanese civilians," Axis History Forum, 28 May 2007. Available at: forum.axishistory.com//viewtopic.php?t=121354 [Accessed 12 Jun 2017].

————. (2009) "Re: Colonel Francis Hayley Bell, internal security," Axis History Forum, 7 December. Available at: forum.axishistory.com/viewtopic.php?t=152391 [Accessed 3 July 2022].

Pelz, S. E. (1974) *Race to Pearl Harbor: The Failure of the Second London Naval Conference and the Onset of World War II.* Cambridge, MA: Harvard University Press.

Probert, Air Commodore H. (1995) "Setting the scene," *A symposium on the Far East War*, Bracknell Paper No. 6, Mar 24, 1995; pp. 9–21. Available at: authorzilla.com/bdVnQ/microsoft-word-bracknell-no-6-far-east-air-war-doc.html [Accessed 6 August 2022].

Reynolds, E. B. (1994) *Thailand and Japan's Southern Advance 1940–1945*. New York: St. Martin's Press.

Rikusenshi kenkyū fukyūkai (eds.) (1966) *Ma-re sakusen* (The Malaya Operation.)Tokyo: Hara shobo.

"Round–up of Japanese," *Advocate*. Burnie, Tasmania, 9 Dec 1941. Available at: Trove: 09%20Dec%201941%20-%20ROUND-UP%20OF%20JAPANESE%20-%20Trove.webarchive [Accessed, 5 September, 2018].

Sanbō honbu henshū, (1967) *Sugiyama memō, jō* (The Sugiyama Memoranda). Tokyo: Hara shobō.

Shimazu, H. (1993) "The pattern of Japanese economic penetration of prewar Singapore and Malaya," in Saya Shiraishi and Takashi Shiraishi, *The Japanese in Colonial Southeast Asia*. Ithaca, NY: Cornell University Press, 1993, pp. 63–88. Available at: jstor.org/stable/10.7591/j.ctv1nhk4j [Accessed 6 August 2022].

"Singapore espionage," (1934) *The Argus* (Melbourne, VC) [9]. Available at: trove.nla.gov.au/newspaper/article/10999935 [Accessed 12 March 2017].

ST Straits *Times,* Available at: eresources.nlb.gov.sg/newspapers/Digitised/Article/straitstimes.

Sugita, I. (1987) *Jōhō naki sensō shidō* (War Guidance Without [Military] Intelligence). Tokyo: Hara shobō.

Tanemura, S. (ed.) (1979) *Daihon'ei kimitsu nisshi* (Imperial General Headquarters Confidential Diary). Tokyo: Fūyō shobō.

Thompson, P. (2005) *The Battle for Singapore*. London: Hachette Digital edn.

TNA (The National Archives, Kew), CAB 23/15/31, War Cabinet meeting, 15 Aug 1919.

———. CAB 23/70/19, Cabinet meeting conclusion, 23 Mar 1932.

———. CAB 24/229, Imperial defence policy, 23 Mar 1932.

————. CAB 80/22/6, War Cabinet CoS Committee report, 6 Nov 1940.

————. CAB 65/8/29, War Cabinet meeting, 1 Aug 1940.

————. CO273/644/9, Japanese in Malaya, Dr Tsune Ouchi.

————. Records of the Security Service, KV3—The Security Service.

————. KV3/251, Serial 9 a, 1–9, NA. The *Wani* Maru.

————. KV3/251 Japanese espionage activities in the East Indian Archipelago and Straits Settlements and India (1934 Jan 01 – 1938 Dec 31).

————. KV3/252 Japanese espionage. Activities in the East Indian Archipelago and Straits Settlements and India (1934 January 01– 01–1938 Dec 31).

————. KV3/415 Japanese espionage case in Singapore, December 1935 (1934 Aug 01 – 1935 Mar).

————. KV3/416 Japanese espionage case in Singapore, December 1935 (1935 Apr 02 – 1941 Feb 26).

————. KV3/426 Japanese intelligence activities in Malaya (1940 Jul 11 – 1955 Mar 16).

Tomohito, E. (2005) "*Senzen no kaiyō shōnendan no shidōsha yōsei*," (Training of prewar leaders of the sea scouts), Kyūshū daigaku daigakuin kyōikugaku kō-su insei ronbunshū (Kyushu university graduate school in education graduate student thesis). Available at: catalog.lib.kyushuu.ac.jp/handle/2324/3680/KJ00004183271. pdf [Accessed 18 June 2017].

Tomono, R. (1983) "'*Mare-no tora' Harimau shuzai kikō*" (An account of collecting materials for 'The tiger of Malaya'), *Reikishi to jimbutsu, zōkan Taiheiyō sensō-kaisen hiwa*, (*Rekishi to jimbutsu, special issue*, The Pacific war—unknown episodes), pp. 136–143.

Tsu, Y. H. "Japanese in Singapore and Japan's southward expansion, 1860–1945: Historical notes for under another sun,"

Asian Educational Media Service, Available at: aems.illinois.edu/mpg/sun/tsu.html [Accessed 18 March 2017].

Tsuji, M. (1993) *Japan's Greatest Victory: Britain's Worst Defeat*, translated by Margaret E. Lake. New York: Sarpedon, edn.

Tsushima, M. (2000) "Emperor and world renewal in the new religions: The case of Shinsei Ryūjinkai (Part 2)." Available at: kokugakuin.ac.jp/ijcc/wp/cpjr/newreligions/tsushima.html [Accessed 20 February 2020].

Walton, C. (2013) *Empire of Secrets: British Intelligence, The Cold War, and the Twilight of Empire*. New York, NY: Overlook Press.

War History Branch, Department of Internal Affairs. (1963) *Documents relating to New Zealand's participation in the Second World War, 1939–45*, vol. III, Appendix IV—"Appreciation by the United Kingdom Chiefs of Staff on the situation in the Far East, 12 August 1940." Available at: nzetc.victoria.ac.nz/tm/scholarly/tei-WH2-3Doc.html [Accessed July 9, 2022].

Wigmore, L. (1957) *Australia in the War of 1939–1945*, Vol. IV, *The Japanese Thrust*. Canberra, AU: Australian War Memorial 1st edn.

Yamamoto, F. (2016) *Nichi-Ei kaisen e no michi* (The Road to the Outbreak of the Japanese-English War). Chūōkōron shinsha, Inc.

Yoshimura, A. (1981 edn.) *Daihon'ei ga furueta nichi* (The Day That Shook Imperial General Headquarters). Tokyo: Shincho bunkō edn.

Yuen, C. L. (1978) "The Japanese community in Malaya before the Pacific War: Its genesis and growth," *Journal of Southeast Asan Studies*, 9(2), pp. 163–179.

Zadankai (1983) (Roundtable discussion) "Mare-oki kaisen to 'chuko' no tatakai," (The battle of the Malaya sea and 'medium' bomber' battles), *Rekishi to jimbutsu, bessatsu, Taiheiyō sensō – kaisen hiwa*, pp. 349–366.

Recommended further reading

Few American historians display interest in pre-war Japanese espionage in Singapore or the subsequent Malaya military campaign. British and Australian historians have produced several excellent book-length military histories, but only a few short articles deal specifically with pre-war Japanese espionage. Japanese historians tell of military espionage but write little about either Japanese residents or the Foreign Ministry's intelligence roles. Singapore historians tend to write about the wartime Japanese occupation or post-war Singapore. The social history of the Japanese community in pre-war Singapore remains relatively unknown although a recent grant to the Asian Research Institute (ARI) hopefully will remedy that omission in the coming years.

Further information is available at: https://ari.nus.edu.sg/grant/mapping-middle-road-prewar-japanese-community-in-singapore [Accessed 1 Sep 2022].

Index

www.ingramcontent.com/pod-product-compliance
Lightning Source LLC
Chambersburg PA
CBHW070346270326
41926CB00017B/4012